forty
days
with
the
enemy

forty
days
with
the
enemy

RICHARD
DUDMAN

liveright
new york

to Helen, Janet, and Martha

1. 987654321

Standard Book Number: 87140 − 537 − 7
Library of Congress Catalog Card Number: 70-157097

DESIGNED BY MADELAINE CALDIERO

Manufactured in the United States of America

contents

1	capture	1
2	investigation	22
3	flight	32
4	revolutionists	45
5	invitation	63
6	attack I	78
7	comrades	95
8	attack II	121
9	cleared	130
10	farewell	150
	epilogue	176

our five guerrilla escorts

Hai, a veteran revolutionary, probably a North Vietnamese, the political leader of the group.

Ba, a soldier in the National Liberation Front of South Vietnam, the military commander of the task force.

Tu, also a South Vietnamese in the NLF, who looked after our personal needs.

Wang, a Cambodian student of Chinese descent, only two years with the revolution, bookkeeper and purchasing agent for the task force.

Ban Tun, a Cambodian army officer who defected and joined the revolution the day before the overthrow of Prince Sihanouk.

forty
days
with
the
enemy

1
capture

It was five minutes at the most from the time we first suspected that we were in trouble until a slim Vietnamese guerrilla stepped from behind a tree, pointed his Chinese-made repeating rifle at us, and took us prisoner.

Beth was the first to notice that our borrowed car was the only moving thing in sight in the flat Cambodian countryside.

"Doesn't it seem awfully quiet?" she asked.

Mike and I agreed that the highway seemed strangely deserted for noontime on a sunny day in early May. No peasants walked the dirt path on the shoulder between the asphalt and the sunken, dry rice paddies that stretched off to the horizon. No babies cried, no children played, no dogs barked around the occasional farmhouses along the main route from Saigon to Phnom Penh.

The last person we had seen was a lone Cambodian sentry two miles back at the outskirts of Svai Rieng, where some oil cans partly blocked the highway.

"Are there more troops ahead?" Beth had asked him in French.

"Yes."

"May we go on?" she had asked.

"Yes, but it is *inutile*."

An odd word, and he may have meant it as a warning.

We should have taken the look of Svai Rieng as a warning, too. But it had been exactly noon, and I had jumped at the conclusion that the place closed down promptly for lunch. Our biggest problem had seemed at the time to be catching up with the invading American and South Vietnamese troops that we thought we were following.

With Beth's remark, it began to dawn on us that we had blundered into no-man's-land—if that term can be borrowed from the old conventional wars, where battle fronts were well-defined, combatants mostly wore uniforms, and where most people could agree on who were friends and who were enemies. In the second Indochina war, already nine years old, there was no front. The American forces and those of the Saigon, Vientiane, and Phnom Penh regimes controlled the air and the major cities in South Vietnam, Laos, and Cambodia and could go almost anywhere else in the daytime. But Communist-led guerrillas roamed the countryside at night and hid in the daytime. Most of Indochina was no-man's-land. We three correspondents—Elizabeth Pond of *The Christian Science Monitor*, Michael Morrow of Dispatch News Service International, and Richard Dudman of the *St. Louis Post-Dispatch*—had gotten ahead of the invading column we thought we were following and had gone beyond the temporary reach of the force on the American side.

We knew for sure that we were in trouble when, a moment after Beth had sensed that we were alone on the landscape, we found our way blocked by a blown-up bridge. There was no barricade or warning sign, just the collapsed span with slabs of pavement slanting steeply down to a creek underneath. Mike, a cool driver, turned the car around deliberately and headed it back toward Svai Rieng.

We had gone no more than one hundred yards or so when a young man in a blue sport shirt stepped from behind one of the broadleaf trees that lined the highway. He pointed his ·AK-47 at us and barked something in Vietnamese. Mike quickly brought the car to a stop. We scrambled out with our hands up. Mike, who speaks Vietnamese fluently, told him: "We are not soldiers. We are international journalists. We are not Americans. We are Canadians."

A young Cambodian, carrying a similar rifle, joined the first guerrilla. They ordered us to put down our cameras and empty our pockets on the pavement.

"Turn around."

"I'm afraid you'll shoot us," Mike said.

"I won't shoot you," the guerrilla said. "Turn around and march down the road with your hands over your heads."

Mike passed these orders on to Beth and me, and we started walking.

My own feelings were a mixture of anxiety and excitement. I knew that there was some chance that we would simply be shot and buried in a shallow grave. I recalled pictures of the bodies of a German doctor and his wife whom I had known in Hue. They had been found that way after the city had been retaken from the Communists in 1968. Like the Germans, we had been captured in the heat of battle. Hatreds were running high, and even the coolest enemy commander could decide that innocent civilians were a dispensable burden.

The date was significant. It was Thursday, May 7, 1970, six days after President Nixon's announcement that he was sending American ground forces into Cambodia to destroy Communist sanctuaries in the frontier area and thus safeguard American troops remaining in South Vietnam. It was seven weeks after the coup in which Lon Nol and Sirik Matak had overthrown Prince Norodom Sihanouk and converted Cambodia from a neutralist buffer state into an ally of the United States and the Saigon regime.

I knew that there was a good chance that we would be suspected of being part of the invading force. The car we had borrowed the night before in Saigon looked something like a military Jeep, even though it was painted a bright blue and was a civilian International Scout.

But the three of us looked entirely unmilitary. Mike's red hair had grown long, and we both had grown medium length sideburns. My bald head showed that I was too old to be a soldier. I was fifty-two, Mike was twenty-four, and Beth was thirty-three. None of us had on any of the army clothing often worn by American correspondents. Mike wore a striped broadcloth shirt and black pants, Beth a light print blouse and tight-fitting black pants. She had a brown silk scarf tied around her ponytail. Beth and Mike both are nearsighted and wore thick-lensed glasses. Both had on leather sandals. Except for my brown cordovan oxfords, I could have been dressed for golf or tennis: white polo shirt with a little alligator emblem on the chest and white duck pants. None of us ever carried weapons.

Beyond that, we all had been personally opposed to the Vietnam war for a long time. I am optimistic by nature and felt elated at the prospect of getting my first look at the other side of a war I had been writing about for ten years.

As we walked along in the humid midday heat, after climbing down one side of the collapsed bridge and up the other, we all began to feel less nervous. After all, we had survived the crucial first few minutes and were still alive. Now all we had to do was convince the guerrillas that we were truly civilian newspaper correspondents. Mike and I were walking together ahead of the others. "If we get out of this alive," I said, "we'll have one hell of a story."

Mike tried to strike up a conversation in Vietnamese with the blue-shirted guerrilla and got as far as asking where he was from. "Ben Tre," the young man replied. That is the place in South Vietnam of which an American colonel once said, "We had to destroy the village to save it," thus providing a capsule characterization of American strategy for years in much of Indochina. The guerrilla's answer suggested that he might have a special reason to hate Americans. It also told us that he was South Vietnamese, probably a member of the Viet Cong or, more properly, the National Liberation Front of South Vietnam.

Suddenly in the distance we heard the throb of a helicopter. *"Di! Di! Di!"* ("Hurry! Hurry! Hurry!") the first
guerrilla shouted. We ran, still holding our hands over our
heads. There was no cover except for the green line of
broad-leafed trees along the roadside. Some of them had
been felled and lay across the highway as makeshift road-
blocks. Brown dry paddies stretched into the distance,
separated by green grassy dikes and an occasional grove of
tall coconut palms.

"Throw away your passport," Mike whispered. I had
kept my blue U.S. passport in my pocket, not wanting to
contradict his lie that we were Canadians by dropping it on
the pavement with the rest of our belongings. Now, I
decided against disposing of it, quickly balancing the
hazards of being identified as an American against those of
being caught trying to conceal my nationality.

I was getting winded. "I don't know how long I can
keep this up," I told Mike. Beth was lagging behind. Two
or three other guerrillas on bicycles had joined us from
hideouts somewhere along the road. One of them gave her
a lift on his rear luggage rack, and she passed us with a big
smile.

After about two miles, we were ordered to turn off
down a side path and to halt in front of a thatch-roofed
hut. A half dozen men and women appeared. Mike and I
were ordered to take off our pants and the three of us to
take off our shoes and sandals and toss them to one of the
men. He motioned for us to sit on a low bench while he
went through our pockets and examined our shoes and
sandals. He tossed them back after removing my passport
and a small pocket knife and handkerchief. He handed

back my glasses. As we put on our clothes, a black-eyed Cambodian woman, her head covered with a checked cloth tied into a loose turban, brought a brass basin of water and set it before us, saying something in Vietnamese. "We can wash our hands and faces," Mike said. The splash of the cool water was agreeable. Another woman brought a battered china teapot with a wire handle and poured unsweetened hot tea into three small glass cups.

After a few minutes' rest, we were ordered to sit sidesaddle on the luggage racks of three bicycles that had been brought into the dusty yard. Three young men then pedaled us another half mile along a pathway to another hut—this one on stilts—with about twenty persons crowded under the elevated floor. Most of them were armed men, the rest women and children. It appeared to be a forward command post. We sat on a crude bed made of three branches, and our first interrogation began.

"Who are you?" a young man in a red shirt asked in Vietnamese.

"We are international journalists," Mike replied. "I am Canadian, and so is she" (pointing to Beth) "and he is an American" (indicating me). I had told him that I wanted to be identified as an American rather than trying any tricks.

"What are you doing here?"

"We came from Saigon this morning. We drove along Highway 1 into Cambodia to observe and report the results of the invasion by American and Saigon forces. We didn't know that we were entering liberated territory."

"Whose car is that?"

Mike told him that we had borrowed it the night before

from an American friend in Saigon and that it was not a
military vehicle. The car belonged to the Saigon representative of the Committee of Responsibility to Save War-
Burned and War-Injured Vietnamese Children.

There was a pause. This first examination seemed reasonable enough. "We'll have to have a reunion sometime
when this is all over," I told Mike and Beth. "Right now,
Mike, you'd better tell them to give us our pens and
notebooks. We've got to start being reporters."

But another questioner took over. The first had spoken
with an air of authority, but he deferred to an older man,
possibly forty-five, with one eye that was just a scarred
socket. We had noticed him earlier, scowling and im-
patient. He wore a khaki uniform without insignia.

"We think you are agents of the CIA," he told Mike in
Vietnamese.

"That's not true. We are international journalists. We
have nothing to do with the United States Government."

"Then what are you doing here?"

Mike repeated the story of our trip from Saigon up to
the time of our capture.

The one-eyed man listened without comment, then
turned away and began superintending an inventory of our
belongings, including our overnight bags that had been
brought from the car. There was no sign of our typewriters. When the guerrillas came to my roll of Vietnamese
currency, One-eye asked how much it amounted to. I
guessed thirty thousand piasters, which I had changed the
day before in order to pay my bill at the Continental
Palace Hotel in Saigon. Another held up Mike's camera,

pointed to a crack in the filter and asked whether it had already been damaged.

"It's only the filter," Mike said. "The lens is not hurt, and I probably did it myself when I put the camera on the pavement. It doesn't matter."

A young man noticed my watch. "I want to borrow this," he said and began taking it off my wrist. I told Mike: "Tell him to go ahead, but tell him that watch was a present from my father on my twenty-first birthday, thirty-one years ago." I don't know why I thought that would make any difference or whether Mike translated it or not; he sometimes censored me when he thought it wise. I assumed that the watch was going to be considered loot, but after some discussion it was noted on the inventory and was put into Beth's plastic bag along with our money and cameras.

A young woman in a flower printed sarong with a cloth tied over her hair led Beth up a ladder to the main floor of the house. They returned a few minutes later, Beth had been directed to undress and had been searched. The respect shown for Beth's privacy seemed a good sign.

A young Cambodian who spoke some French told Beth that he was a student from Phnom Penh who had been "permitted" to join the revolution, a privilege usually reserved for trained soldiers. He was interested that she had spent several months in Czechoslovakia. But One-eye spoke sharply to him in Vietnamese. The friendly chat abruptly ended, and the young man moved away.

A Cambodian guerrilla entered, wearing a khaki U.S. Army brush hat, with the letters "F.U.N.K." on the front of the upturned brim. We guessed correctly that the letters stood for the *Front Uni National du Kampuchea*, the United National Front of Cambodia, the new political movement headed by Prince Sihanouk and backed by Hanoi.

An older man approached the house, a Vietnamese of perhaps forty-five, his grey hair standing up in a long brush cut. After quizzing One-eye, the newcomer put us through another interrogation. The same questions, the same answers. Who were we? When had we left Saigon? Why had we entered "liberated territory?" He frowned as if in disbelief at every reply of Mike's. There was a long discussion in Vietnamese.

"Can you ride bicycles?" the one-eyed officer asked Mike. He said we could, and presently the three of us rode off single-file with an escort of four guerrillas, rifles slung over their shoulders, along a dirt path that made right-angle turns as it threaded its way between rice paddies.

We pedaled about two miles until we reached a standard 2½-ton army truck parked on the paved highway that ran through another village. Its canvas top and hood were covered with freshly cut branches. We could see the name *Skoda* on the back, indicating that it was one of the Czech trucks that had been supplied to Sihanouk's army when he still was the Cambodian head of state and had been taken along by defecting soldiers when he was ousted.

Two men slanted a plank against the back of the truck and ordered us to walk up and climb over the tailgate into the body of the truck. "They say to sit down on the floor and don't look outside," Mike said. We crouched on small blocks of wood we found lying near the front of the truck bed. A half dozen Cambodians, most of them in their twenties and armed with rifles, carbines, and one light machine gun, mounted after us and stood guard as the truck lurched off down the highway.

One of our guards was pointing his AK-47 at my chest. In a reflex reaction, I motioned to him to point the muzzle to one side, forgetting that I was in no position to make any suggestion. He raised the barrel so that it pointed straight at my head and held it there for the rest of the ride.

I judged by the sun's direction that we were going north and west. The Cambodian student, who had joined the guards as an interpreter, had switched from amiable intermediary to proud warrior. He leaned out the back of the truck at every hamlet and village, holding up three fingers and shouting something that included the word "American." Mike's story that he and Beth were Canadians had been ignored, and we were being heralded as captured Americans. At two villages, we slowed down, and I caught a glimpse of a temporary wooden archway decorated with flowers and pink and blue plastic ribbon, with a framed photograph of Sihanouk mounted at the top. At one point, someone stepped onto the running board to make sure that the branches of our camouflage would clear it. There was a brief stop each time to let the people look at the captives.

At a third village, the end of our ride, the villagers had fifteen or twenty minutes to take turns climbing onto the cab or tailgate to gape at us. Men and boys and an occasional woman would climb up, glare fixedly, and shake their fists. One young man reached out with his upturned hand in a clawing, ripping gesture as if to castrate us. An older man with hollow cheeks and staring eyes climbed to the cab roof and began shouting and gesturing with a downward motion of his open hand. "He says to lie down on the floor," Mike said. We quickly lay face down, hands outstretched. This seemed to drive the man into a greater frenzy, until Mike decided that all he wanted was for us to sit on the truck bed instead of on the small blocks of wood.

The villagers were close to becoming a lynch mob, when a young Vietnamese, in military uniform but without insignia, came aboard and ordered them off the truck. He, too, asked who we were and how we came to be captured.

"You are not going to be shot," he said. "But we must blindfold you before we take you off the truck." Strips of Turkish toweling were bound over our eyes and tied at the backs of our necks, so tightly that they pulled our chins down to our chests.

Someone took me by the hand and helped me over the tailgate and down a plank to the ground. Mike, Beth, and I gripped each other by the hand. I told myself that the blindfolds were a security precaution. Beth thought they meant something else. "I don't think it's come to that," Mike told her.

But Mike thought he heard a Vietnamese voice say, "One must kill prisoners of war." He told Beth to start talking again to the Cambodian student, and we could hear her telling him in French once more that we were not military people. Mike dropped the name of an acquaintance he had in the North Vietnamese delegation in Paris, who could vouch for his identity. The name seemed to mean nothing to them.

We were grasped by the wrists and led through a gauntlet of villagers. We could hear them yelling and could feel an occasional fist in our backs. Then Beth's hand was wrenched away from mine, and the hands holding Mike and me began pulling us along a rough path or road. *"Di! Di! Di!"*("Go! Go! Go!"). For the first time I really feared that we were being led to our execution, but it seemed best to concentrate on the one thing we could do anything about—putting one foot ahead of the other. "Be careful not to turn your ankle," I told Mike. We were still holding hands to protect each other from falling.

There was a brief halt. Someone tied a slip knot of binder twine around our outside wrists. *"Di! Di! Di!"* said the voice, and we heard the sputter of a motorbike. It moved and we moved, pulled along as fast as we could run. Voices shouted, fists prodded us to speed us up. Mike kept encouraging me and shouting in Vietnamese, "My friend is fifty-two years old. He can't keep running this fast." It didn't help. I pumped my legs, puffing hard, saying over and over to myself, "I must not trip. I must not turn an ankle."

We stumbled along for a half-mile or more when the voices of the villagers died away and I could feel the path trailing off into heavy dust or sand. There flashed into my mind a scene at Hue after the Tet offensive, the mass graves I had seen in 1969 in the dunes outside the city, where the Communist forces had executed several thousand civilians and had dumped their bodies into shallow trenches. I was certain that the same thing was going to happen to us. The thought did not frighten me so much as it puzzled and disappointed me. I thought to myself: "I'm right in the midst of my life. There are so many things I still want to do. Now it looks as if the whole thing will be over in the next minute or two."

The motorbike stopped. Someone tied another piece of toweling around my eyes, and I felt fingers punching the edge of the cloth into my eye sockets to make sure I could not see. Still holding hands, Mike and I were led forward a few steps. My foot kicked a threshold, and the deep redness beneath the blindfold changed to black as we moved out of the afternoon sunshine into darkness and a room with a dirt floor.

Suddenly I heard a sharp "crack!" and felt Mike sink to the ground with a groan. I thought he had been shot and that I would be next. But it was a wooden club, and it smashed down on the back of my head a moment later, knocking me to the ground. I lay there, still blindfolded, expecting to be kicked or beaten, but, as Mike told me afterward, someone ordered in Vietnamese, "Don't hit them again." I was pulled to a sitting position, my wrists lashed together behind my back, so tightly that the rope would have stopped the circulation if I had not strained against it as the knots were being tied. Mike, whom I could feel sitting beside me, said, "They want us to spread our legs." As we sat waiting for whatever was to come next, I heard in the distance what seemed a high-pitched shriek of a woman in pain. I was sure Beth was being tortured. Along with the anxiety over what I thought was happening to her and shortly would happen to us, I soon felt excruciating discomfort sitting upright with my legs spread straight out and with nothing to support my back. All I wanted at the moment was to lean back against something or at least cross my legs.

A man's voice barked questions at Mike: "You're American spies, aren't you?" "You are agents of the CIA, aren't you?"

"No," Mike said in a pleading tone. "We are international journalists. We have no connection with the United States Government or with this invasion of Cambodia. We are trying to tell our readers the truth about the invasion. Our only interest is in truth and peace." He repeated that he knew a member of the North Vietnamese delegation to the Paris peace talks, who could vouch for his identity.

"My friend is the chief of the Washington Bureau of the *St. Louis Post-Dispatch*, one of the great newspapers in America, one that has opposed the Indochina war for many years. And our colleague is a correspondent for *The Christian Science Monitor*, another great American newspaper. She has written many articles against the American aggression in Indochina. I am a correspondent for an independent news agency, Dispatch News Service International."

There was no response. We thought we heard the crunch of footsteps walking away. Mike whispered a translation of their exchange.

"How badly hurt are you?" I asked.

"Not seriously," he answered. "I was knocked out for a few moments, but I don't think anything is broken. But I'm worried about the circulation in my hands."

I told him they must have hit a hard place on my head and it didn't bother me much.

Another voice, also in Vietnamese but this time soft and compassionate, sounded unexpectedly, close to our ears.

"Are you afraid?"

"Yes," Mike said. "I don't know what is going to happen to us. Have I reason to be afraid?"

"Not if you are really journalists. Would you like a drink of water?"

"Give it to my friend—he's older," Mike said.

I felt the edge of a metal cup at my mouth and gulped several big swallows. It was one of the best drinks I have ever tasted.

"He says we can lie back against the sacks behind us," Mike said. "It will be more comfortable. And we can cross our legs if we like."

"Are the ropes too tight?" the man asked Mike. He said they were, and the man quickly loosened them, then loosened them again when Mike said he still could feel no sensation in his hands.

"It isn't polite to do this to you," the voice told him.

"Are you a captain?" Mike asked.

"No, just a lieutenant."

He was silent a moment.

"Now get ready to go," he said. "You will be able to bathe and wash your clothes, and you will be given something to eat."

He pulled me up by the arm and led me out of the building, along a path for a few yards, and into another building. I could feel a cement floor under my feet. I was guided carefully across the room until my shins touched a bench. We were told we could turn and sit down.

Then we heard Beth. She had been brought in at about the same time and was helping the Vietnamese officer untie our wrists and take off our blindfolds.

Through a partly opened door, we could see that it

already was nearly dark outside. The light of a little kerosene flame showed Beth, smiling at the reunion, and the kindly lieutenant, a slim, thin-faced soldier of perhaps thirty-five years. He had on a khaki colored pith helmet, khaki shirt and pants, and blue-and-white rubber shower sandals.

"We are going to be fed," I told Beth, "and we can have a bath and wash our clothes."

A Vietnamese brought in a five-gallon gasoline can of cold water and Mike's and my bags. In the dim light, we could see that we were in a schoolroom, with a few long benches pushed against the walls and a long table next to our bench. The guerrillas shifted a blackboard on an easel over into one corner as a makeshift screen and set the water behind it, indicating that we could bathe there. They handed us a bar of laundry soap and left.

Beth bathed first, using Mike's washcloth and towel. She had to put on the same shirt and pants, grimy from the road dust and the guerrilla truck. Mike and I had each brought a change of clothes. Unzipping my small blue Pan American flight bag, I found that it contained not only my spare polo shirt, khaki pants, underpants, and socks, but also my toilet kit, small pocket knife, and an extra pair of glasses.

In turn, we washed, using a dipper to rinse off the soap. One of the men brought another can of water, and Mike offered to wash his and my dirty clothes. He did the best he could. The water was cold. I asked Beth how she had been treated.

"Not badly. The student told me that you and Mike were being taken away for questioning."

She had been removed to another room and seated, still

blindfolded. She could hear villagers coming in for a look at the Western woman prisoner. Someone shouted angrily at her in Cambodian, snatched off her sandals, and threw them against a wall.

Later, left alone with a guard, she asked for water, drank it, asked for more, and got it. Taking courage, she had untied her blindfold. She was in a schoolroom. A young Vietnamese stood guard near the door. He walked over to her and pulled her silver rings from her fingers and made a timid effort to seduce her. "This is not necessary," she said, "you are my brother and I am your sister." Her words were in English. He put the rings back on her fingers and made no more trouble.

The thin-faced lieutenant soon appeared and told Beth she could lie down on a table if she wanted a nap. He said that his superior officer had just learned of our capture and had sent him to make sure she was not being mistreated. Not long after, another soldier picked up her sandals and escorted her across the schoolyard to the room where we were being taken.

It must have been nine or ten o'clock. We had set out from Saigon at dawn. Mike and Beth had not bothered with breakfast. Two Vietnamese brought in a black pot partly filled with steamed rice. It was still warm, apparently left over from the guerrillas' dinner. Beside it they set a side dish of fried cubes of pork fat, a pot of tea and three glasses, three plates and three tablespoons. We all had two or three helpings, sitting side by side at the school table.

The thin-faced soldier, who was becoming a familiar figure, stepped into the room as we were finishing and said that some other men were coming to talk to us. As we stood up, three men walked in, led by a tall Vietnamese—about five feet ten, tall by Vietnamese standards—with an erect bearing, eyes set wide apart, and a big mouth that broke into the beginning of a smile as he greeted us. He wore khaki pants and a khaki military shirt with straps on the shoulders and open at the neck. He was about forty. He spoke in what Mike afterward told us was a pure North Vietnamese dialect. He described himself and the other soldiers there as ethnic Vietnamese (thus avoiding the issue of nationality), who were fighting as part of the pro-Sihanouk revolutionary front in Cambodia.

At his request, Mike repeated our story. The tall officer nodded in recognition when Mike gave the name of his North Vietnamese friend in Paris.

"If you are truly international journalists, you will be released," the officer said. "If you are agents of the CIA, you will be treated according to the law of the country. You will be taken to a safe place while we are checking on you. It is not safe for you here. The Cambodian people do not know that there are good as well as bad Americans. They know only the tanks and planes of American imperialism. So you are not safe among the Cambodians. I have assigned this officer" (turning toward the thin-faced lieutenant) "to be responsible for your safety. Stay close to him and you will be all right."

This gave us our first hope that we eventually would be released. There was a sharp reminder, nevertheless, that we still were prisoners suspected of being spies. As we sat on our low bench opposite the guerrilla soldiers, I crossed my knees to get into a more comfortable position.

"Sit up straight with both feet on the floor," one of the younger men barked at me.

When the tall officer finished his instructions, he told us to rest; he and the others filed out. We lay down side by side on our backs on the bare cement floor.

Perhaps an hour later, all but the tall officer returned and we were ordered, "Get ready to go." We packed our wet clothing into the bags and filed out into the moonlit night, across the schoolyard and along a winding dirt path toward a waiting British Land Rover, something like an oversized Jeep with a small curtained truck body at the rear.

A sad-faced young man with a broad-brimmed World War I-style army hat, blue shirt, and green pants took the lead, holding his AK-47 by the barrel with the stock resting on his shoulder. We followed. The thin-faced man and several others brought up the rear. One attracted my attention as we climbed into the back of the car and bumped off along dirt roads through the night. He was a stocky young Cambodian, taller and heavier than most of the Vietnamese we had seen, with a broad face and full lips and a mouth full of gold teeth.

We rode for an hour or so, with occasional stops when a flashlight would shine briefly from the woods alongside the road. One of the soldiers in our crowded car would shine an answering flash, and dark figures would move out from among the trees for whispered conversations with our escorts.

We stopped in front of a well-built house, on the customary stilts with a ladder leading up to the front door. The pink of a tile roof and smooth walls of milled lumber showed in the moonlight. After our escorts had whispered with the Cambodian man of the house, we were ordered to hurry up the ladder. The sad-eyed soldier directed us to a large room in the back of the house, separated by tall cupboards and wardrobes and a door of hanging pink and blue plastic ribbons. Inside were two wooden chairs and a big wooden bed that had rigid strips of wood in place of springs and mattress, with a straw mat laid on top.

"Rest," the soldier told us.

Beth said, "I think I'd like to sleep in the middle."

We guessed it was 2 or 3 A. M. We lay down and fell asleep after one of the longest days of our lives.

2
investigation

The first daylight was filtering through the broad leaves of the banana palm outside our window when the slight, sad-faced young man of the night before, still wearing his blue shirt and faded green pants, stepped into the room and told Mike in Vietnamese, "It is time to bathe."

He said "Madame" could go first and that Mike and I could go out one at a time after she had returned. She took the towel and washcloth and our bar of soap and followed him out through the silent house and down the front ladder to the ground. When it was my turn, I followed Beth's directions and went first to the toilet area, a shallow ditch a few yards down a path through the close grove of low banana palms. The soft brown dead leaves made a good substitute for toilet paper.

Near a back corner of the house was the bathing place, a tin basin on a tree stump next to a waist-high pottery jar nearly full of clear water. Beth had left the towel and soap in the crotch of an old fence post. The splash of the cool water reminded me of a similar improvised washroom I had used in 1960 in a little village in Laos, on the first of many assignments to Indochina. Cold water is good enough in that tropical climate.

The same young man brought us breakfast, with a shy smile but not yet any start at conversation. He put a blackened brass pot, a third full of rice, on the foot of the bed, with three china soup plates, three tablespoons, and a steaming pot of tea with three little glass cups without handles. The rice, left over from the guerrillas' breakfast, was still warm. It was lightly milled—nutritious, I judged —and the grains were firm but tender. It made a satis-factory breakfast.

The first day began in a friendly way. Anh Tu—we had heard the others calling him "Brother Tu" the night be-fore—returned after breakfast with three sarongs and a plastic bag containing three toothbrushes and three tubes of Cambodian toothpaste. He said the sarongs would give us a change of clothing. Each was a long tubular skirt of printed cotton, and we soon discovered how to hold it up by taking a big tuck to make it fit snugly around the waist and then rolling over the top a time or two to make it hold tight.

During breakfast, and as we examined our new belong-ings, we had our first visits from the Cambodian family that lived in the house. The mother, a tall, handsome, black-eyed woman, probably in her late twenties, came in and unrolled a new woven plastic mat on top of the straw mat where we had slept, to provide another quarter-inch between our backs and the hard boards. She wore a sarong and blouse and a checked scarf folded to cover most of her straight black hair. We had no way of talking to her, but we smiled as she used a rag to brush some grains of rice down between the slats on the floor and carried out our dishes. She smiled tentatively, with cautious hospitality.

A moment later, her little daughter, about four years old, poked her head in between the pink and blue plastic ribbons that formed the door to our room. She looked like a little oriental doll with her black eyes and carefully trimmed bangs. When we smiled, she scurried back but presently approached the door again, seemingly pre-occupied with grabbing a handful of the plastic ribbons and letting them fall back in place one by one but actually getting a good look at the three round-eyed Westerners. The father kept his distance. We could see him dimly, moving about in the front of the house or lying on one of the beds.

Tu came in again, this time with a pot of mid-morning tea. Mike and I hurriedly put on our shirts as a mark of courtesy. We had stripped to the waist as the heat and humidity had begun to rise. He asked us to sit down and then was silent as he poured a few drops of tea into each glass, swished it around, poured it out through the slats of the floor, and then poured a cup for Beth, a second for Mike and me to share, and a third for himself.

"Did you have enough to eat?" he asked.

We told him the rice was excellent and added that the tea was especially welcome because the heat had made us thirsty. We asked if we could drink what was left of the water he had brought us in a basin for a morning wash.

"If you drank it you would get sick and die," he said.

Death often figured in his conversation. He took us through the story of our trip into Cambodia in his mild, compassionate-sounding way and then, when we told about the moment of capture, he said, "You are lucky to be alive. If you had had guns in the car you would have been killed immediately."

There was another interval when we were left alone. Then Tu returned and told us we would have a visitor, someone from higher up who was coming shortly to ask us some questions.

"The important thing is to tell the truth," he said.

A caricature of a Communist counterintelligence agent entered the room. He was a small man in khaki with a scowl and rigid bearing that bespoke self-importance. He wore a pistol at his waist and a khaki dispatch pouch over his shoulder. His preliminary drink of tea was a quick gulp, without the usual nicety of sipping it together and a few minutes of small talk.

"Why did you come here?" he asked. His southern accent indicated he was a Viet Cong.

Mike went once more through the story of the day before up to our capture. He described us as "international journalists" and said we had had those words pasted on our windshield in Vietnamese.

"Then why did the American helicopters come and broadcast a request to help three American government agents escape from the liberated zone?"

Mike had not heard of any such broadcast and said he had no idea why we would be described in that way.

"What is your connection with the CIA?"

Mike said that we had no connection at all with the CIA. He repeated that we were independent news correspondents and once more described the *St. Louis Post-Dispatch*, *The Christian Science Monitor*, and Dispatch News Service International.

The glowering little interrogator went around and around with his questioning, jerking his head impatiently as an indication that he believed nothing of our story.

The barked questions and Mike's replies were in Vietnamese, and Beth and I had to follow them at the time by the occasional word we could catch. Mike concentrated intensely on each word of each question and answer, watching the interrogators lips to catch the full meaning and putting his replies in begging, almost whining tones of painful sincerity.

After a half-hour of this, the interrogator grunted to signal an end of the session, and he and Tu went out. Mike was exhausted, and he had to lie down for a few minutes before he could give us the details of the exchange and join us in considering where we stood. Mike was deeply disturbed by the hostile attitude and evident disbelief shown by "Ironface," as he began calling him.

After massaging Mike's back and shoulders for fifteen minutes to loosen him up, I decided that we would have to do something to ease the burden. There would be more interrogations, and it would be too much for Mike to bear the whole load. I proposed that we string out the next session by having him translate each question into English so that Beth and I could help formulate the answer. This would break up the machine-gun pace that had been such a strain on Mike. It also would help prevent Mike from making some quick reply that might be mistaken as an admission that we were spies. We would have to watch our words carefully. Mike suggested that one of the guerrillas might understand English, and we decided that we must be cautious even when speaking among ourselves.

We agreed that one possibility was that we were being prepared for a frame-up and a show trial as CIA spies. I found it hard to accept such a hopeless prospect and began arguing that the manner of the inquiry and the questions asked were really quite reasonable, no worse than what would happen in an American investigation and far better than some of the third-degree methods employed by the South Vietnamese. We guessed that we were getting our first taste of the old hard-and-soft system used by investigators everywhere, with Tu as the soft one, posing as our friend, and Ironface as the tough one, trying to intimidate us into admissions.

By this time we guessed that it was early afternoon. We were being left to ourselves. Through the curtained doorway we could get an occasional glimpse of one of the guerrillas or members of the Cambodian family napping or talking quietly. It promised to be a long and idle day, possibly the first of a great many of them. Passing the time would be a problem, with no books and no paper on which to make notes.

We began to think constructively about how to get through this thing in the best shape possible. Regular exercise was one requirement, and we did a few bend-downs for a starter. Mike offered to teach Beth and me to speak Vietnamese, and one of our first sentences was, "If you please, I wish you would do me the favor of letting me write a letter to my family." It was a sentence we planned to use when Tu returned and there was an opening for the request. And then Beth came up with a brain teaser that was to occupy Mike's and my spare moments for a week. It was the puzzle of the twelve silver balls, all the same in size and appearance and all but one the same weight. The question is how to identify the odd ball and tell whether it is lighter or heavier than the others by using only a pair of scales and making only three weighings.

"Don't ask me to tell you the answer," she said. "I won't do it."

Presently, as we talked, the little girl crept inside the doorway and listened solemnly to our voices in the strange language. Then we got to see her brother, about six, who came in on an errand, looking for something. In Cambodian, he asked us where the *ptadl* was. We guessed correctly that it was the small brass pot we had been given as a urinal and pointed it out, back in the corner beside a tall wooden wardrobe. He made a face as he marched outside to dump it.

The shadows outside were long and the light in our room was dim when Tu came in with still another member of the household, a girl of about nine, slim and black-eyed, wearing a cotton blouse and a checked sarong around her narrow hips. "Her parents were killed yesterday by American planes," he said. "These people have taken her in."

He gave us some pages from a blank school notebook and said we were to write the answers to some questions as part of the investigation.

After giving our full names and addresses, names of members of our families, and names and addresses of our newspapers, we were to list the dates of all visits we had made to Paris, Saigon, Phnom Phen, and Laos and give the dates and descriptions of all articles we had written from each place. Then, what newspapermen did we know in each of these places? Had we made reports to the CIA? And, finally, what persons could we name who would vouch for us? Beth, whose French was the best, was to translate these dossiers into French, and we were to sign them. We had been permitted to keep two ball-point pens, and Tu lent us a third.

We asked if we could write letters to our families. He said we could and left us to get started.

We went right to work, first on brief letters home. I hoped to get word to my wife, Helen, and to head her off from any plan she might have had to fly to Saigon or Hanoi.

Getting started on the dossiers, we considered it impractical to list all our articles about Southeast Asia since we all had spent so much time there and had written so much. The key questions seemed to be the one about the CIA, which of course called for a flat denial (I added that I felt it would be a conflict of interest for a newspaperman to have a side activity as a part-time intelligence agent), and the requests for names of people we knew. We all tried to recall names that might be familiar to our captors and might put us in a favorable light. I listed Wilfred Burchett, the Australian journalist who has spent much time in Hanoi and with the Viet Cong in South Vietnam; Harrison Salisbury, the *New York Times* editor whose reports from North Vietnam in late 1966 first told Americans about the true nature of the U.S. bombing raids; some foreign diplomats, including some from neutral and Communist countries; leaders of some of the organizations opposing the Vietnam war, and Senators Fulbright, Mansfield, McGovern, and McCarthy.

We worked most of two days on the writing task, including Beth's translation into French, and handed Tu the dossiers and our letters home. Another day passed, and Ironface was back. He pulled the papers from his pouch and flipped through them like a stern teacher dealing with lazy pupils.

"They are not long enough and they are not neat enough," he said. "You must do them again, and it is important that you tell the exact truth."

There was another series of questions, mostly repetitious of what he had asked us the first time. The device of translating them into English helped ease the tension. The only crisis came when Ironface asked if any of us was familiar with the *Chieu Hoi* program, the so-called "open arms" program in which the Saigon government tries to persuade members of the Viet Cong to defect by offering them a bounty and amnesty after a short rehabilitation course. I told him that I knew something of *Chieu Hoi*, having in mind several stories I had written through the years questioning the official line that increasing number of these defectors meant the war was being won. I had written that many of them are not defectors at all but merely ordinary citizens who want the bounty or want to escape the draft and that others are Viet Cong who pass through the rehabilitation procedure as a sort of rest and rehabilitation program and then go back to being guerrillas. But Ironface leaped on my answer. Had I been to

Chieu Hoi headquarters? Whom did I know there? Too late, I guessed that he had in mind another aspect of the program, the intensive investigation of these defectors by Saigon counterintelligence agents. I minimized my knowledge of the matter as best I could.

When Ironface finally left, Mike was gloomier than ever. "I can see what is going to happen," he said. "He's going to use the old Chinese method of making us write this thing over and over forty times and keep looking for contradictions." It seemed possible. Ironface had kept our first drafts, and the second would have to be from memory. I had found it hard to remember the dates of my seven assignments to Southeast Asia, and I would find it hard to list them exactly the same way a second time.

Mike's suspicions had made us all uneasy. As we went to work on our second drafts I made up my mind to try to keep my worries to myself and do what I could to keep up our spirits.

It would not be easy. Tu came back in and took Mike out for a separate interrogation that lasted fifteen or twenty minutes. Mike returned with new cause for alarm. They had told him that a United Press International report of our capture, heard on the radio, used our names but said nothing about our being news correspondents. They said it called us "American agents." It could not have been true, but Mike hesitated to accuse them of lying about it. Instead, he said that we were well known to the UPI reporters and editors and could not understand how such a report could have been broadcast.

If that was their game, we wondered what would come next.

3
flight

We must have been sleeping lightly the third night when someone entered our room. We sat up in bed and saw Tu's hollow cheeks and sad, kindly eyes by the tiny flame of his kerosene lamp. He said, *"Chuan bi di."*

"Get ready to go," Mike translated. We stuffed our few clothes and toilet articles into our bags. Tu told us to drape our sarongs over our heads and led the way out through the house and down the ladder. Someone had looked after my shoes and had set them at the base of the ladder.

The moon was bright and the air was cool. We must have slept several hours. I felt refreshed and looked forward to a night march. Tu led the way, his broad-brimmed hat square on his head and his AK-47 held by the barrel across his shoulder. We three followed him single file, and

there were three or four other dark figures behind us. No
one spoke. We took a curved path around the edge of a
wood next to a flooded rice paddy. As we drew away from
the house, something up above caught my eye. I saw a man
perched two-thirds of the way up a tall coconut palm. The
glimpse of a lookout reminded me that we were in the
hands of an organization that owned the night.

But our hike lasted only a few minutes. We heard the
sound of an engine idling and came to our Land Rover,
parked and ready for us. We were ordered in first and
found seats on a bench over one of the rear wheels and on
a crate on the floor. Between us and the driver's seat we
could see the dim outlines of packs and bags of supplies.
When I tried to tuck my feet back under me, they bumped
against two rifle barrels.

Tu got into the front seat with some others. The thin-
faced soldier who had halted the beating the first night sat
beside me, the pistol on his belt jabbing me in the hip. His
sharp features were expressionless under the brim of his
khaki pith helmet. He ignored us. Across from him I could
recognize the husky Cambodian guerrilla by his size and
his broad face and full lips. As he lit a cigarette, I could see
the flash of his gold teeth. He set the stock of his carbine
on the floor of the car and held the weapon between his
knees.

The putt-putt of a motorbike approached. Through the
open back of the Land Rover we could see the bike and
driver, with a guerrilla with a rifle strapped across his back
riding behind. They led the way, and our car bumped off
along the narrow road. Without appearing inquisitive, I
tried to keep track of our direction by glancing out from

time to time as we made a series of right-angle turns to
check the position of the moon or the direction of the
north star. We traveled mostly north and west, but I found
it impossible to judge distance, since there was no way to
tell speed or elapsed time.

It was a quiet ride. No one spoke while we were in
motion. From time to time, as on the first night, the beam
of a flashlight would shine out briefly from a clump of
trees, and one of the guerrillas in the car would answer
with his flashlight. We would stop, and several dark figures
would approach the car for whispered conversations.
Sometimes we would wait, while the motorbike went
ahead, presumably to scout the road. Sometimes we would
hear the clink of bottles and judge that the gas tank was
being filled from old wine bottles, a common practice all
over Southeast Asia. Sometimes, after one of the quiet
consultations, our car would turn around and start off in
just the opposite direction, and we would know that our
captors had missed a turn.

In the distance, sometimes to the left and sometimes
behind us, phosphorus flares lit up the horizon. U.S. Army
units often fired the flare shells, with their bright charges
that float slowly down on parachutes, throughout the
night to help detect any enemy effort to overrun or
sabotage an outpost. These could have been from the two
new firebases inside Cambodia that I had visited by helicopter a few days earlier, where U.S. forces had cleared the
jungle and set up artillery pieces.

Presently we began to overtake long lines of figures
walking single file along the side of the road. Some were
women and children, carrying heavy packs, pots and pans,

and sometimes squawking chickens with their legs tied together. The car stopped several times, and the two guerrillas in the back helped Cambodian women with babies climb over the tailgate and find seats on the bench or on the floor. Eventually I counted sixteen persons in the car. Sometimes the walking figures were guerrilla soldiers. In the dim light I could see their rifles and carbines. They seemed to be dressed in no particular uniform. I could not guess whether they were Vietnamese or Cambodians. Some hobbled along on makeshift crutches made of tree branches. Whenever the car would slow, the soldiers would run after us, hoping to hitch a ride. The thin-faced man waved them off, but he did take some of their packs, stuffing them into every spare space left in the car.

What we were seeing was a mass flight of Cambodian villagers and guerrilla troops getting out of the way of the American and South Vietnamese invading columns along the eastern frontier. Once I counted two hundred of the soldiers. At another place we passed fifty or sixty lying down for a rest stop alongside the road.

We could see only gimpses of the countryside. Sometimes one of the flares would be reflected in a broad series of flooded rice paddies that stretched off to the horizon. Sometimes our road would go through a jungle so thick that vines and branches would brush the canvas roof of the car. Sometimes I could see a row of whitewashed fence posts and guessed that we were passing one of the French rubber plantations.

It was still dark, and we had driven maybe two hours, maybe five hours, when we stopped in front of a big wooden house, and the thin-faced man told Mike that we were to cover our faces with our sarongs. Peering through the folds of the cloth, we could see a dozen guerrillas and villagers talking. Someone pointed a flashlight inside the car. Thin Face ordered everyone away from the back of the car. The peasant women got out with their bundles and their babies, and we passed out the soldiers' packs to be stacked on the ground. Tu came around to the back and told Mike we were to hurry out of the car and up the ladder into the house.

It was a barn-like building, and we were led to a separate room in the back. The bed this time was several broad three-inch planks laid side by side on two sawhorses. Tu and a Cambodian boy unrolled two mats, and the boy brought us each one of the little Cambodian pillows, which are about the size and shape of a large brick and almost as hard. We were tired and stiff from the ride and went right to sleep.

The Barn, as we called the place, looked dusty and deserted. After the usual dawn trip outside, we could see on the wall the faded pictures of a man and woman and their children, dressed in Western clothes, and out in the big open front room, where several guerrillas still slept on the floor on straw mats, a tall desk strewn with school notebooks where a schoolmaster could have stood or a landlord could have kept books on his tenants. Straw mats shuttered the windows, so that we could see out only through narrow cracks. One improvement was our own water supply—a big clay jar full of water, with a brass *ptadl* on the wooden cover.

We began to settle into a daily routine. The cool early morning was a good time for exercises. I did bend-downs, some stretching and breathing movements, and a few push-ups. Beth worked hard at riding a bicycle on her back with her legs in the air but sometimes just stood and swayed her shoulders gently in a twisting motion that I told her did no good at all. Mike, a tall, husky, twenty-four-year-old, shook the house by rocking vigorously on his stomach with his back arched and doing as many as fifty fast push-ups in a row. He said he had been a long-distance runner at Dartmouth, and I felt better about getting so winded in the blindfold run the first day.

After breakfast, the usual steamed rice and tea with some bits of stewed meat as a side dish, we worked on our dossiers, taking an occasional break to talk or to work at learning Vietnamese. The language class led to a minor incident. A Cambodian boy in a white shirt stood at the door frowning at us for a few minutes and then told Mike reprovingly in Vietnamese, "This is not Vietnam. This is Cambodia." Mike told him we hoped to learn Cambodian, too, but the youth just turned and walked away.

Occasionally we could hear gunfire and bombing in the distance. Sometimes it would be the tenor drumbeat of machine guns, sometimes the heavier pairs of explosions that meant artillery fire. In the morning and evening we often could hear and feel the deep, irregular booms of the huge bombs dropped by the B-52s, each of them powerful enough to blast a hole the size of a house.

The roar of airplanes often sounded in the distance, and several times the *blat-blat-blat* of a helicopter came close to the house. Twice we scrambled under the bed, lying on the dusty slats underneath and hoping that if there were shooting the heavy planks would stop the bullets.

In the late afternoon, Tu came with the rice pot and the teapot. Then there was another session of writing, trying to remember the dates and places of everything we had written about the war and trying to recall the names of additional references around the world. Finally, the evening trip outside, one at a time, and a chance to wash a pair of shorts and a sweaty shirt. More writing, by kerosene flame, and it was time to go to sleep.

It was in the Barn that Beth had her first menstrual period since our capture. Mike had difficulty explaining the problem to Tu, since Mike's Vietnamese vocabularly was out of balance. In Vietnam, he had been using the language mostly to discuss politics, and he knew such phrases as "non-Communist opposition" and "American imperialism" but had difficulty with simple words like "blood" or "cloth." Tu at last got the point—"Oh, it's what the Vietnamese women do every month!"—and brought a roll of coarse gauze bandage. Beth used my two white handkerchiefs one at a time, fashioning a pad by wrapping one of them around some folds of gauze and fastening it together with two safety pins I found in my toilet kit. She handled the matter so simply, washing out the handkerchiefs in the *ptadl* and hanging them up to dry on a piece of string in the far corner of our room, that I'm afraid she made less fuss than Mike and I did about our shaving. We had only my reel-type safety razor—the guerrillas had taken away our older-type razors that took a two-edged blade—and it had only three more turns left in the cartridge. I still had a stick of shaving soap, but the brush was gone. We decided against growing beards, afraid of offending the guerrillas, who always were clean shaven, kept their hair closely trimmed, and never wore a trace of sideburns. We agreed that by shaving every two or three days we could stay reasonably neat and still stretch out the blade and soap in the event it was a long captivity. We knelt one at a time on the floor, using Mike's hand mirror and the brass *ptadl*, and cleaning out the razor afterward with a sliver of bamboo.

Ironface returned one afternoon, after we had turned in our dossiers, accompanied by a younger man who spoke French and had the annoying habit of holding one palm over his mouth whenever he spoke. Ironface, speaking to Mike in Vietnamese, went through the same skeptical questions he had asked before. Mike again slowed the pace by translating the questions into English. The other man, meanwhile, spoke with Beth in a steady monotone, telling her reproachfully that it was essential that we tell the exact truth about ourselves and observing that our cameras were "very peculiar," not the sort that journalists would carry.

Ironface took a harder line than usual. By this time I had heard enough Vietnamese to recognize his North Vietnamese accent, with its harsh "z" and "v" sounds.

"We are considering you as American personnel," he told Mike.

"What does that mean?" he asked.

"You are United States Government personnel. We are not yet sure whether you are CIA, military, or refugee" (presumably he meant American officials assigned to encourage enemy desertions), "but we are treating you as American personnel."

We still weren't sure what this meant, but it sounded as

if we might not even be granted prisoner of war status, much less accepted as news correspondents. There seemed to be a strong possibility that they would execute us as spies.

The session was unsettling as usual, and afterward we considered the fact that the dangers seemed to alternate. Sometimes we would be menaced by American planes and artillery, sometimes by some new hint by our captors that we were going to be treated as spies. The enemy was sometimes Viet Cong, sometimes American.

We left the Barn in a hurry on about the third afternoon, when it was clear that the present danger came from the Americans and that we and the guerrillas had a common interest in escaping from it. With Tu leading the way as usual, we walked single file across a series of dry rice paddies divided by lines of palm trees and an occasional small palm grove. We could hear helicopters in the distance, and I complained to Mike that we really could be walking faster. But the guerrillas seemed to know what they were doing. As we approached one of the groves, I saw a lookout perched in a palm tree and a freshly-dug trench just inside the outer tree line. We waited under the trees while the thin-faced man reconnoitered ahead.

When he had returned with word that it was safe to go on, we crossed more open country to the next scattered cluster of houses. We were led up to the first one, a thatch-roofed shack, and up a ladder and into the dark main room. In the gloom, we could see the Cambodian family huddled inside the doorway while we were motioned off to the right into a windowless, screened-off storeroom, where the family's best straw mat had just been

unrolled for us. Fifteen minutes there, and then on by
motorbike one at a time along a dike path to a big new
house, the thatch clean yellow and the floor made of
springy golden strips of bamboo, laid with the polished
outer side up. The Cambodian farmer and his wife ignored
us, but a teenage daughter only pretended to be busy with
her sewing and then put it aside to crouch close to our mat
and watch our faces as we talked quietly.

There was yet another move that day, another walk to
an old shack where an old Cambodian man smoked his
marijuana cigar with a palm-leaf wrapper and admired
Mike's physique as we did some exercises. As darkness fell,
the old man told us the Cambodian words for parts of the
body, including a special name for each bone of each
finger, until Tu came and quietly asked him to go outside.
We guessed that he thought the familiarity had gone far
enough.

Tu told us what had been happening: "American and
Saigon tanks and helicopters attacked the house where we
were staying. They killed the whole family and destroyed
the house. We are safe here for a while. They will wait
there for two or three days before coming farther."

Mike thanked him for getting us away so skillfully.

"If we had not, you would be dead by now," Tu said
without expression.

Every second or third night after that we would move
again, traveling in the Land Rover, which the guerrillas had
somehow been able to save from the advancing Americans
and South Vietnamese. The days we spent in a succession
of houses to which we gave names like Jungle House and
Bug House to keep them straight in our memories. Jungle

House was a dirty little thatch-roofed shack with palm-leaf mats for walls and a hole the size of a book for a window. A heavy afternoon rainstorm started a chorus of hundreds of bullfrogs. When Mike and I went outside at dusk, ducking twisted branches, huge leaves, and tangled vines until we reached the edge of a muddy pond, the sights and sounds seemed bigger than life—more like a Disneyland version of a jungle. The grunting and snuffling of a sow that was penned directly underneath where we slept added another strange touch.

The Bug House was a big tile-roofed structure, with a single enormous room except for our little screened-off bedroom in one corner and a kitchen at one end. We gave it the name because of thousands of black bettles that continually crawled up the walls and clung to the roof tiles until thunder or a distant B-52 raid would cause them to begin dropping like light rain on the mat, on our heads and into our food. Beth, at 33, is a very self-possessed young woman, and her devotion to Christian Science seemed to have helped her withstand pain and annoyance. The nearest I saw her come to cracking came at the Bug House. Despite our efforts to shield ourselves from the falling beetles by putting some of our few sheets of writing paper over our food, one of them dropped into her rice bowl just as she was about to take a bite. For a moment there was real anguish in her voice: "Oh, I'm so miserable!"

A strange sense of timelessness began to affect us. To keep the days straight, I would announce the day of the week and day of the month each morning and we watched for something unusual to mark each Thursday, which meant the passage of another week since our capture. Part

of our problem was that we had no idea of our captors'
plan of action or even whether they had a plan. The route
seemed to be strangely inconsistent insofar as we could
judge, sometimes north, sometimes south, sometimes east,
sometimes west. Were we trying to thread our way to some
base camp or possibly to Laos and on up to Hanoi? Or
were we just running this way and that, trying to stay clear
of the ground and air attacks?

We kept looking for signs of what was to become of us.
Sometimes we saw indications where there were none and
worried unnecessarily. One night at the old man's shack,
Beth went out first to bathe, escorted by the Cambodian
guerrilla. She was gone for what seemed a very long time. I
began to wonder at what point we should go after her and
what we could do about it if they had mistreated her. Mike
must have had similar thoughts as we waited in silence.
Then we heard her voice as she returned after one of her
leisurely baths in the moonlight. I told Mike, "We'll have
to be careful about letting our imaginations run away with
us."

Another indication looked like a sign for the good, and
it turned out to have real substance. One night when we
were bouncing along in the Land Rover, with Anh Ba, the
thin-faced lieutenant sitting beside me on the side bench,
we came to one of our sudden stops. The usual shadowy
figures slipped up from the roadside to the car. The big
Cambodian guerrilla climbed out, and Ba prepared to follow him to confer with the sentries. In a completely
off-handed manner, he unbuckled his pistol belt, laid the
belt, loaded pistol, and ammunition on my lap, and
jumped out of the car. If he had spoken English, I would

have expected him to say, "Would you hold this a minute, Mac?"

We were alone in the back of a car loaded with rifles and carbines and a machine gun or two, and now I had a loaded pistol lying in my lap. I wasn't sure whether they trusted us, thought we didn't know how to handle a gun, or just felt sure that we were too smart to make a break. Possibly they were testing us. At any rate, we had come a long way from having rifles pointed at our heads that first afternoon.

4
revolutionists

Gradually we came to know the guerrillas in our little task force as individuals.

Tu, the sad-faced young man with the blue shirt and green pants who was in direct charge of us, would sometimes sit and talk for a few minutes when he brought our breakfast or dinner or an occasional snack. Sometimes he offered bits of incidental information. Once, when he brought some slices of French bread and a saucer of thick, sweet condensed milk, he told us the bread was from Vietnam. "We are near the border, and some of our people brought it for a treat," he said.

Once when we had been answering his questions about who we were and how we had come to Cambodia, Tu told me unexpectedly, "If you really are the chief of the Washington Bureau of a great newspaper, I am proud to know you." He must have meant it; he was too gentle and serious for sarcasm.

Another time he sat down cross-legged beside us and asked in his quiet, mournful way, "Do you miss your families?" It sounded like a sympathetic question, and Mike replied, "Yes, we miss them very much."

"I have been away from my family for eleven years. I haven't seen or heard of them since then," he said. "A month or two is not a long separation."

How were we to read a remark like that? Was it an admonition not to feel sorry for ourselves because their hardship was so much greater than ours? Was it a hint that after a month or two we would be freed? Or was it just a way of telling us something about himself?

It appeared to be the last. His reference to his family apparently was to his parents, somewhere in the Mekong Delta in South Vietnam, because after sitting silent a moment he went on to say that his wife had been killed a few weeks earlier in a massacre of Vietnamese by Cambodian government troops at Prasaut, a city through which we had passed on our way into Cambodia. Their infant daughter had been taken somewhere else to live with friends, he said.

Anh Ba, the military leader of the task force, always with a trim khaki uniform that matched the fine lines of his thin face, said little but he sometimes would squat next to our screened-off area and offer Mike a Cambodian cigarette, light it with his Zippo lighter, and sit there smoking for a few minutes. Despite his silence, we came to think of him as one to trust in time of trouble. He was always alert, always the first to hear a distant helicopter. Our lives could depend on his military competence.

We sometimes heard the guerrillas call each other by their real names, but we thought it best to go along with their usual practice of using these security nicknames. Anh Ba means "third brother," and Anh Tu means "fourth brother."

The Cambodian soldier had no such nickname. For his own protection, Mike and Beth and I decided to give him one in whatever we wrote about him. We decided to call him Ban Tun, which means "good man" in Cambodian. Through one of the Vietnamese guerrillas who could speak Cambodian, Ban Tun told us that he had been an officer in Prime Minister Lon Nol's personal guard until the day before the March 18 coup when he had quit to join the revolution. He had left his pregnant wife in Phnom Penh, where they had a house and automobile, he said. He wore two small figures of Buddha on a rope around his neck under his shirt.

He was strong and took obvious pleasure in his strength. He often wanted to match the others in Indian wrestling, and he always was the one who forced the other's arm to the floor. In the morning, Beth noticed how he would bound to his feet and then look around to see if anyone was watching him. She admired his powerful shoulders and strong, square face, remarking repeatedly that he would be a good sculptor's model.

Ban Tun seemed to rank lowest in our little task force. He wore no pistol and was usually the one to build the fire or haul water from the well. Mike thought at first, with

some resentment, that the others treated him as an Uncle
Tom. Most of our exchanges with him in the first two
weeks were in mimicking each other's words. One night
when we had been riding for hours, he taught us the
expression, *hot nuh*, saying it over and over, with heavy
emphasis on the last syllable—"*hot NUH*"—as if he were in
agony. Finally we figured out that it meant "tired." He
taught us to say "drink tea" in Cambodian and then
worked hard to learn the English expression. At first it
came out "br-r-rink tea," but we coached him until he got
it right. It was hard for him, and we kidded him afterward
about being *hot nuh*.

A fourth member of the team, whom we shall call Wang,
was of mixed Vietnamese and Chinese stock. His fluent
Cambodian supported his story that his home was in
Phnom Penh. He said he had been with the revolution for
two years. One of the others told us that he came from a
wealthy family. He was friendly, without saying much.
Once he heard Beth singing an air from Mozart, and he
whistled a bit of it and explained that he had studied
Western music. He was in his late twenties and unmarried.
Wang was the quartermaster of the outfit, and he often
would make out a shopping list on a tiny piece of paper
and set out on a motorbike for a nearby town, his rifle
strapped on his back, to buy tea soap, salt, sugar, pepper,
and maybe some new flashlight batteries. Soap sometimes
could not be found, but we never were without the food
staples.

Those four, two experienced Vietnamese soldiers, a
Cambodian defector, and a Vietnamese-Chinese Cambo-

dian with limited experience, were, of course, hand picked to guard us and escort us and thus could not be considered a random sample of the guerrilla army. Yet they had been selected within an hour or so in the immediate vicinity of where the truck had deposited us unexpectedly the first night. We could feel that they had some value as a sample of the hundreds of others whom we saw but could not come to know.

The fifth member of the five-man task force joined a week later, obviously sent from a higher headquarters to take charge of us ideologically; that is, to examine us and undertake whatever reeducation was required.

Anh Hai (second brother) arrived one day accompanied by an extremely thin, slightly hunched soldier who had a pronounced twitch of his left eye and cheek. With them was a Vietnamese photographer with a good Japanese 35-millimeter camera. We were in the jungle house at the time. The two soldiers sat cross-legged at the entrance to our dark alcove. The blanket that had been hung over a rope to screen us from view had been pushed partly aside, and a succession of young Vietnamese guerrillas and Cambodian men, women, and children peered curiously at us as we talked. The photographer squatted behind the soldiers, snapping shot after shot in the gloomy twilight. Unless he had very fast film they were worthless.

It was another interrogation session, but with a difference. Hai was a chubby-cheeked Vietnamese with greying brush-cut hair and an alert, intelligent expression. He seemed fully aware of the respect due his age and rank, so much so that he could ignore them. Instead of quizzing us, he began chatting with us, as if he wanted to get acquainted rather than make another try at getting us to trip ourselves in telling our story.

He expressed interest when I said I knew Wilfred Burchett, observing that this could be a help in resolving our case. The photographer, a talkative, ingratiating type, told us that he, too, knew Burchett, having escorted the Australian journalist on one of his ventures into South Vietnam with the Viet Cong. They wanted to know if we had met Michèle Ray, the French fashion model and free-lance writer who had been captured and spent several weeks with the Viet Cong in South Vietnam; I had reviewed her book, but none of us knew her.

Taking out his cigarette papers and pungent country tobacco, Hai offered Mike a smoke and rolled one for himself, then told us something of his background. He said he had joined "the revolution" twenty-five years ago as a nineteen-year-old peasant with three years of schooling. That made him forty-four and a veteran of the fighting against the Japanese (when Ho Chi Minh was for a time an ally of the United States), the French, and now the Americans. He said he had fought in one hundred battles and had been wounded four times. He told us that he had long since learned to live with the danger of war, even the thunderous bombardment from the B-52s.

"Once you have experienced the B-52 you do not fear it again," he said. "We do not fear any of the American weapons. We have an intuition that tells us where the B-52s will strike and we move away."

Crouching forward on his hands and feet, he rocked gently back and forth to show us how he had learned to ride out the pounding of the huge bombs. He said he had been through three of the B-52 raids.

How much of this was bravado and propaganda and how much was true, we had no way of knowing at the time. If he was speaking the truth, it would help explain why the strategic bombers have fallen far short of expectations in the Vietnam war and why the men and supplies have continued to flow along the Ho Chi Minh trail from North Vietnam through the Laotian panhandle and into Cambodia and South Vietnam despite the thousands of tons of those blockbusters that the United States Air Force has dropped on this system of infiltration routes.

With Hai's arrival, we began to feel less isolated and in a better position to learn something from our experience as captives. Another change came a few days later, on May 19, the day after we had reached the big house where the black beetles dropped from the ceiling. Hai brought a steaming china pot, decorated with a picture of a deer and a fat Chinese, and asked us to join him for a cup of tea. He must have thought we needed cheering up.

"You know, there is nothing to be sad about," he said. "Once we have taken a person prisoner we never kill him. War is not to kill people but to win a cause. We believe that bad people are just misled. Bad Americans just don't understand. We don't like to kill Americans, not even American soldiers. We know that they don't understand our situation. Anyone can be educated. When we capture someone, that is the end of our difference with him."

We knew that the North Vietnamese and the Viet Cong had executed prisoners on occasion, notably the two or three thousand Vietnamese shot and dumped into mass graves outside Hue during the Tet offensive of 1968. But we knew also that the killings at Hue were committed in the heat of battle, at a time when the Communist forces held the city against fierce American attacks that were gradually closing in and eventually retook the old capital. There had been accounts of some American servicemen found shot to death with their hands tied behind them, but these could have been exceptions to general practice. I was willing to accept Hai's assurance at face value and take it as good news for us. He had stopped short of saying that we had been classed as good Americans, but his words were the first authoritative assurance that we were not going to be killed.

May 19 was important in 1970 for another reason. It was the day when the birthday of Buddha, which moves about the calendar like Easter, coincided with the birthday of Ho Chi Minh. After our usual late-afternoon dinner, eaten among the falling beetles in our little windowless screened-off room, Tu invited us to go out into the main part of the house. We sat drinking tea on the supple bamboo slats, darkened and polished by many bare feet, next to a broad open window looking out at the leaves of banana and mango trees with a glimpse of bright blue sky beyond. Through an open door at the far end of the big house we could see tall coconut palms and the well where we had bathed in the darkness the evening before. The man of the house, a tall, greying farmer, sat quietly next to the open front door, smoking a banana-leaf cigar of marijuana and sipping tea from a small pot kept warm in a cozy made from a coconut husk; there wasn't much for him to do at the moment but wait for the beginning of the rainy season, the time to plow the paddies and plant the rice. Outside on the front porch other Cambodians, including a handsome dark-eyed woman far into pregnancy whom I took for the old farmer's daughter, talked quietly with the Cambodian Ban Tun and some of the Vietnamese guerrillas. The light and air and the quiet, peaceful scene revived our spirits still more.

Tu squatted down beside us.

"Do you know what day it is today?" he asked. "It is the birthday of Bac Ho. Do you know who Bac Ho is?"

Mike was taken aback. He said afterwards that he felt as chagrined as if he had forgotten Passover at the home of a Jewish friend. He said of course he knew who "Uncle Ho" was.

We had moved down to the end of the big open room, next to the open door where a soft cross-draft felt cool and pleasant.

Tu had brought us a treat for the occasion, a small brick of sweetened popped rice, which is a holiday specialty in Vietnam. Vendors with pushcarts take a charcoal fire and a hollow iron popper along the street, and children run out with the rice and sugar and a few piasters to have him make the confection.

"We all wanted to bring Uncle Ho to Saigon while he was still living," Tu said. "We were not able to do it, and we feel very bad about that. So we struggle harder now to make it up to Uncle Ho. We commemorate his birthday by fighting harder for the freedom and independence of our country and against the American aggression."

From his shirt pocket, he took a small red book and showed it to us. On the first of the thick brownish pages, in old-fashioned Vietnamese characters, was the title: *A Short Biography of Ho Chi Minh*. Inside the front cover was a picture of Ho.

He said: "We all have these. We read them from time to time to remember Uncle Ho and all he has done. He could have been the leader of international Communism after Lenin, but he chose to return to Vietnam to make the revolution to liberate his people. We continue that revolution, and we will be victorious. It is certain. The revolution will be successful. When we have defeated American aggression we will go home. Until that time, as long as one of us is left, we will fight on."

Hai joined us and began talking about Vietnam's wealth in natural resources, in minerals, and timber as well as agriculture. He promised a bright future for his country, once it was peaceful and reunited. Bringing the conversation back to Ho Chi Minh, he told us of Ho's emphasis on practical education as distinguished from ivory-tower intellectualism. He said that Ho had once questioned an agricultural engineer as to what time of day was best for watering and fertilizing growing plants. The engineer did not know. He told him that the right time was the morning and then warned him against learning that drew him apart from the practical needs of the people.

By that time it was nearly dark, and Tu had lit one of the little kerosene lamps. Its flame and another next to the old man at the front door were reflected on the polished slats of the floor, showing the even rows of joints where six or eight slats had been cut from the same bamboo tree.

It was time to bathe, Tu said, and tonight the three of

us could all go to the well together. We could take as long as we liked and wash all our clothes.

Later, Hai watched with amusement as I rigged a tent arrangement in our room to keep the bugs from dropping onto our faces as we slept. I stretched two long strips of inner tube from one wall to a bench and used Mike's bag and an old flatiron to secure the loose ends there. After watching me spread our sarongs on top, he went to his knapsack and got out his carefully-folded plastic tarp and helped us lay that over the strips of rubber instead. It provided considerable protection, and we spent a reasonably comfortable night. The Bug House didn't seem so bad after all.

The sessions with Hai became regular affairs. One morning a few days later, before we had ventured out into the main room, he squatted at the door of our little room, offered us tea, invited Mike to roll a cigarette for himself, and began a chat that turned into a broad discussion of Communist strategy in the Indochina war. Mike hunched close to him to watch his lips and catch the tones of the subtle language. He translated into English a few sentences at a time.

Mike asked him why it had been so quiet for the last day or so. We had not heard the usual boom of bombs and artillery, and there had been only an occasional drone of an observation plane in the distance.

"The Americans have left for another place," he said. "The American strategy in Cambodia is easy for us to counter. They all stay together, and when they go to a place we go somewhere else. We just stay out of their way.

We are happy when they use up their ammunition and fly their planes. It does not hurt us, and it is expensive for them."

Hai repeated an earlier assertion that the government in Phnom Penh would have fallen already if American and Saigon forces had not invaded Cambodia to prop it up. But in strategic terms he declared the invasion was to the advantage of "the revolution."

"First," he said, "the invasion has brought the Cambodian and Laotian peoples into a unified struggle, together with the Democratic Republic of Vietnam and the National Liberation Front of South Vietnam, against the American aggression. Second, it has drawn American and Saigon troops out of South Vietnam and made it easier for us to fight the Americans there. Finally, it has made new difficulties for Nixon in the United States. It has strengthened the opposition in Congress and among the students."

"Our strategy is to use few men to oppose many," he said, calling attention to a reversion to this standard guerrilla warfare that had followed the heavy Communist losses in the 1968 Tet offensive. So successfully did the Communist forces employ the dispersal strategy in Malaya and later in South Vietnam that it came to be axiomatic that government forces had to outnumber the guerrillas ten to one to gain a military advantage over them. As they gained confidence in South Vietnam, the Communist leaders began consolidated actions involving battalions and even divisions, culminating in the 1968 effort to seize Saigon, Hue, and other major cities. The move was a military failure since it did not lead to an expected general uprising against the Saigon government, but it shocked many

Americans into turning against the war and figured impor-
tantly in Lyndon Johnson's decision to halt the American
escalation and curtail the bombing of North Vietnam.

Hai also told us that when the rainy season began in a
few weeks government representatives and foreigners
would no longer remain with the soldiers, since the soldiers
would stop living with the Cambodian people in their
houses, going out instead into the forest and country side
to begin a military offensive. What this meant about us, I
could only guess. Perhaps we would be taken to some
prisoner of war camp. Perhaps it meant that we would be
released soon. In either case, it surely meant that our
increasingly pleasant life of traveling around with the guerrillas would not last much longer.

I had Mike ask him whether at some point he thought
the Paris peace talks would become important in bringing
about a settlement of the war.

"The Paris talks are like a show," he said. "They are just
a place to make statements that the press can carry around
the world. Nixon would like to break off the talks, because
they continue to call attention to the importance of the
Indochina war, because through them the world is learning
the facts of the American aggression and the truth about
the liberation movement, and because the French people
are hostile to Nixon's policy and the Democratic Republic
of Vietnam has normal diplomatic relations with France.
But Nixon can't break them off, because that would be
too great an affront to the American people and to world
opinion."

He added an unexpected reason why he thought President Nixon could not call off the talks, a reason so subtle

that it made sense only as a typical piece of intricate Vietnamese speculation. He said that to try to shift the talks to another site would remind people of President Johnson's suggestion in 1968 that talks might be held in Phnom Penh, a recollection that now would be embarrassing to the United States because of its invasion of Cambodia.

"Nixon now is in real trouble in Indochina," he said. "He promised peace in six months, and now it's been a year and a half." (Hai was mistaken about the six months; Nixon never had put a deadline on his promise to end the war.) "He's lost the respect of the American people and the American politicians, and he's lost face around the world. He arranged the international conference at Djakarta to try to enlist support for the Phnom Penh government, but that was another failure."

Hai expressed confidence that the revolution would be successful in Cambodia, as well as in South Vietnam and Laos, and reported that Sihanouk's new government in exile already had three cabinet ministers inside Cambodia and many other officials and cadres.

"Sihanouk himself is in Hanoi—he returned there today from Peking," Hai said. (It was about May 22.) "He will not come to Cambodia until the military situation is more secure."

The veteran revolutionist had been speaking very seriously, but the thought of Sihanouk tickled his sense of humor: "He doesn't walk like us—he has to fly," he said with a chuckle. We thought afterward that his laughter was at the thought of the chubby prince trying to walk hundreds of miles along jungle trails. My next question, a reporter's reflexive quest for facts, may have spoiled a chance to lead him into some relaxed talk about what he really thought of this neutralist prince whom Hanoi now accepted as the nominal leader of the new Cambodian insurgency. What I asked was whether Sihanouk would return to Cambodia before the fall of Phnom Penh. He turned the question aside bluntly: "That is a state secret. If I knew the answer, I could not tell you."

Then, as if to offset the seriousness of his reply, he said that talk was a good thing for driving away sadness. This led him to some observations about the joys and sadnesses in the life of a revolutionist.

"A revolutionist either has no family or must leave it behind," he said. "He accepts all the people as his mother, father, brothers, and sisters. When the revolution is won, then he can return to his home place and his family and lead a normal life.

"A revolutionist is sad when the people are poor or when they are oppressed and colonized. But this is not the sadness that makes him do like this" (he buried his face in his hands) "but instead it is the kind of sadness that makes him fight against oppression and colonialism.

"The revolutionist is happy when the people are liberated, when there is a good and improving society, and when the working class is well cared for. This is the exact opposite of the imperialist. He is happy only when he has the control of many countries and can exploit their people and resources for his own interests, when he has many wives, many children, and an easy life."

In our long conversations, usually at night, sitting cross-legged facing each other across the teapot and kerosene

lamp, Hai returned often to the theme of the elusiveness of
his side and its certainty of eventual victory.

"You have traveled with us several times now, at night
in the truck, and you see how we live," he said in one such
talk. "Wherever the Thieu-Ky and American forces are not,
there we are. If there is the smallest space within the
territory they occupy, we fill it. They are nowhere; we are
everywhere. And as long as one of us is left, he will
continue to fight the Americans until we achieve independence for Vietnam, Cambodia, and Laos."

He said confidently that Vietnam would be a rich
nation, selling many products to the Communist countries
of the world. The war had prevented the development of
Vietnam's many resources—he mentioned timber and
minerals—but industrialization and production had gone
forward in North Vietnam even during the bombing raids,
he said.

Another time he told us that we could consider ourselves perfectly safe even though there were American
planes all around and twenty thousand American troops in
that part of Cambodia.

"The troops just stay on the main roads with their
tanks," he said. "They don't come to small places like this.
Our strategy is not to hold any area at all costs but to
retreat and strike where the other side is weak."

Often he quoted the nightly news reports in Vietnamese
by the British Broadcasting Corporation, telling of battles
through much of eastern Cambodia and the frequent de-
fection of entire units of the Cambodian government to
the side of the insurgents. But he predicted no sudden

victory, at least as long as American forces were involved in Cambodia.

Hai relied heavily on the theory of people's war as a recurring theme in his talks with us. He told us once that many Cambodians remained in areas occupied by troops of the Saigon and Phnom Penh governments, "not because they like them, but because they are safe there from the American bombing. They continue to support us and will help us at an opportune time."

We could see for ourselves that relations were good between the Cambodian peasants and villagers and the Communist-led guerrillas from Vietnam. At almost every house where we stayed, a picture of Sihanouk on the wall in a place of honor near the household Buddhist shrine indicated that the family retained its allegiance to the ousted prince rather than supporting the government in Phnom Penh. We saw Wang, the Chinese from Phnom Penh, paying out Cambodian currency for vegetables and meat. Rice, we were told, was contributed by the Cambodian people when they had some to spare; for a few days when we were in an area where supplies were lean, we joined with the guerrillas in getting along on short rations.

The guerrillas reminded us frequently that the country people in Cambodia hated America because of the death and destruction being caused by American ground and air attacks. They said the Cambodians had not learned to differentiate between "good Americans" and "bad Americans" and gave this as the reason why we were kept so carefully out of sight. Once when we were seen by some villagers, the guerrillas explained the presence of Western-

ers by telling them that we were Frenchmen who had
come to help Prince Sihanouk drive out the Americans.
Another reason for concealing us, of course, was to prevent news of our whereabouts from getting back to the
U.S. forces. But the experience that first afternoon, the
glares of the villagers, and the blows and taunts when we
were blindfolded, left no doubt in our minds that the
guerrillas were protecting us from the Cambodians as well
as thinking of their own security and avoiding American
attacks.

Tu gave us a little talk one day about the importance of
cooperation between the guerrilla troops and the people of
the countryside. I asked Mike to tell him that we knew
about Mao Tse-tung's maxim that guerrillas are like fish
swimming in the sea. I had hoped to elicit something that
would indicate his attitude toward the Chinese. But one
should never try to match proverbs with an Asian. He said,
"Yes, but without the fish, the sea is useless."

5
invitation

One morning when we still were living at the big house with the beetles that dropped from the ceiling, Hai asked if we would like to begin writing dispatches even though it had not yet been determined whether we were to be freed. He said the guerrillas would send them to our home offices for publication. It sounded to Mike like a good opportunity to begin behaving more like a news correspondent and less like a prisoner, and he accepted immediately, not waiting to translate the question into English and get a reaction from Beth and me.

I was torn. Any reporter wants more than almost anything else to have a good story of his own on the front page of today's paper. It had been some time since I had had the pleasure. There had been a few pieces out of Bangkok and a few more out of Saigon the week before we were captured, but nothing very special. Before that, I had been on vacation for two weeks in France and Italy with my wife and one of our daughters and had not written a line. A dispatch from captivity would be something special.

But there were disadvantages. There was a real question in my mind whether the *Post-Dispatch* would print an article from one of its reporters while he was being held prisoner. The editors would have no way of knowing whether the reporter was writing freely or being forced to write distortions or even outright fabrications. I had discussed a similar point several times with Marquis Childs, the columnist and my predecessor as chief of the Washington Bureau of the *Post-Dispatch*, in connection with my repeated applications for a visa to Hanoi. He felt strongly that the time to write was after coming out and that articles written from Hanoi would lack credibility. Furthermore, regardless of what the editors thought of them, any dispatches written during imprisonment would, in fact, be written under some degree of duress. I would inevitably be influenced by the knowledge that what I wrote could bear on whether I would be released. I would be involved in a conflict of interest just as surely as a government administrator who has an interest in a firm he regulates or a judge who has interest in a litigant before him. We in the press are harsh in our judgments of such people and could hardly apply a lower standard to ourselves.

I told Mike that for those two reasons I wanted to avoid sending dispatches from captivity. Beth seemed to agree with me, saying merely that she did not plan to send out articles. Mike did not disagree, but he said he felt himself already committed.

He went right to work, using some of the ruled school-book paper that Tu had given us for our dossiers and then some big sheets of cross-hatched graph paper that the guerrillas brought us. He wrote rapidly, first lying on his stomach on the floor, his chest on one of the hard little pillows, then seated at a desk where the Cambodian man of the house had some of his personal papers and where the guerrillas kept their portable radio attached temporarily to the lead from a permanent antenna strung up under the rafters.

Mike's first piece was a good one. It told the story of cooperation and growing friendship that we had seen between the Cambodian peasants and the Vietnamese guerrillas, reporting that the guerrillas paid for the food the peasants supplied them, cooked for themselves rather than having the Cambodians cook for them, and usually lived under the house with the pigs and chickens and farm implements so as not to disturb the Cambodian family more than necessary. In contrast, he recalled a scene we had witnessed at Prasaut the day of our capture. Stopping briefly in the Cambodian frontier city, we had found a platoon of South Vietnamese soldiers with two big army trucks loaded full of chairs, beds, wardrobes, and other household furnishings that had been taken from the houses we could see along the main street, their doors hanging open, stripped bare inside. Other soldiers of the same outfit had backed a third truck up to the municipal rice warehouse and were carrying out the rice and loading it into the truck. One of them took us across the road a few yards to point out a ditch where he said the bodies of one hundred Vietnamese-speaking villagers had been burned after they had been killed in a savage massacre a few days before. The South Vietnamese soldier said his outfit had been too busy to bury them. Too busy looting, he could have said, and Mike made the point in his article.

It was one of those pieces I wished I had written myself. It was straightforward and credible, and I could imagine learning sometime that it had been transmitted to Dispatch News Service International in Washington, offered to newspapers, and maybe printed in the *Post-Dispatch*, while my paper heard nothing from me.

But I stuck to my decision and busied myself with writing a memorandum to Evarts A. Graham, Jr., my managing editor. It was a way of keeping occupied, and, if the memo should be sent to St. Louis, it was the best possibility yet for informing the paper and Helen and my daughters that I was alive and well. When the guerrillas had it translated it into Vietnamese to read it, as I was sure they would before sending it out, it was also a way of giving them a hint as to the sort of thing I would be writing if they would accept me as a correspondent.

Finally, as I began the memo, it occurred to me that it might be quite some time before they knew what I was writing; as far as they knew, I was doing the same as Mike, preparing a dispatch for my paper. The possible confrontation over whether I would or would not write from captivity was thus postponed.

I saved a copy of the memorandum, which was dated May 21, 1970:

To: *St. Louis Post-Dispatch, St. Louis, Missouri,*
   U.S.A.

Memo for Graham:

I am safe and well after accidentally entering liber-
ated territory in Cambodia and being arrested.

I have been offered an opportunity today, May 21,
to write an article for publication. I have replied that I
want to write after current investigation shows that I am
in fact a newspaperman and not a United States Govern-
ment agent.

Members of the Liberation Front clearly have a
relationship of friendship and solidarity with the Cam-
bodian people, and Norodom Sihanouk is overwhelm-
ingly popular in areas we have visited. America and
President Nixon, on the contrary, are hated with a
fervor rarely seen anywhere, because of the American
intervention in Cambodia and the American bombing
and strafing of Cambodian civilians.

I am anxious to begin writing for publication as
soon as possible about this accidental opportunity to
tell about the other side of the war that Nixon now is
widening to include all Indochina. When my credentials
are established, I am told that I will be shown many
aspects of the revolution and I hope to be able to
interview some of its leaders. I do not know how long it
will take to accredit me.

With me are Michael Morrow of Dispatch News

Service International and Liberation News Service and Elizabeth Pond of The Christian Science Monitor.

We are being well treated and protected from the American and Saigon attacks.

I shall begin filing copy when I have been accredited.

"*Regards,*
Richard Dudman

The careful, even stilted wording reflected the habits of speech we had adopted in trying not to offend our captors or cause avoidable crises. It also was the result of a deliberate effort to find words and phrases that would translate well into Vietnamese to be read by Vietnamese Communists. Thus, I was "arrested" rather than "captured." The investigation was to determine that I was not a United States Government agent" rather than a "CIA spy," since the letters "CIA" would have stood out on the page and could have been spotted by members of our guerrilla team. And there was no point in calling them anything but "members of the Liberation Front"; I thought it prudent not to refer to them as North Vietnamese or Viet Cong, since the official story from Hanoi was that none of the Communist forces had entered Cambodia.

Mike wrote three or four dispatches in the next few days, and the three of us settled into a daily routine of spending several hours writing. Beth and I began making detailed notes of our experiences and observations, as well as exact quotations of conversations we had with the guerrillas, while they were still fresh in our minds. Until now, we had been cautious about making notes for fear of arousing new suspicions that we were on an espionage mission. Now that the guerrillas had invited us to start writing, this was no longer a problem. I started off with a full account of the events the day we were captured. Then I wrote an article appraising the American invasion of Cambodia on the basis of what we had seen from our unique vantage point, thinking to have something ready to send off immediately if we should happen to be freed suddenly.

It was datelined "Liberated Zone, Cambodia," and began: "Two weeks after the U.S. and Saigon forces crossed the border into Cambodia, it appears evident from this vantage point that the results will be the exact opposite of what was intended." The "enemy sanctuaries," far from being wiped out, I argued, were being forced to spread out over wider territory with no foreseeable limit on their westward expansion. The bombing and shooting was radicalizing the people of rural Cambodia and was turning the countryside into a massive, dedicated, and effective revolutionary base. Friendly relations were developing between the Cambodian people and the Vietnamese revolutionists "to form a solid revolutionary front with Norodom Sihanouk as its leader and Ho Chi Minh as its hero." Whether or not President Nixon kept his pledge to withdraw U.S. forces from Cambodia by the end of two months, I predicted that Saigon troops would remain in the country and that U.S. bombing and artillery fire would continue. Describing the American invasion as it looked to the Cambodians with whom we had been living, I wrote: "American shells and bombs are proving to the Cambodians beyond any doubt that the United States is waging unprovoked colonialist war against the Cambodian people. They see the United States as a would-be successor to the French, trying to turn back the clock of history in the face of a swelling spirit of Asia for Asians."

Mike turned in several articles, and I handed in my memorandum, which Hai said would be sent along through channels immediately but would take some time to reach the United States because they first would have to be taken somewhere else to be translated from English into Vietnamese so they could be read first. As Mike's dispatches began to flow and my own notes and interpretive articles began to pile up in the bottom of my flight bag, I developed a new cause for anxiety. What if they were trying us out, not to see what we would write if we were freed, but rather to see if we could be converted into permanent captive propagandists for their movement? Perhaps they thought that, with a certain amount of gradual reeducation, along with a mixture of coercion and persuasion, we could be enlisted in their cause as writers or broadcasters like Lord Haw Haw, the Englishman who broadcast for the Germans in World War II. Even worse, in the sense that it would be harder to counteract, was the possibility that Mike was already being drawn into a role that could last indefinitely—writing from captivity articles that the Communist leaders would consider useful and would send out for publication around the world.

In my own case, I thought ahead how to respond if I was urged to begin writing for publication. In the last analysis, I felt I would have to refuse or find myself caught in the same trap as Mike, if indeed it was a trap. I hoped, if the occasion arose, to be able to explain the matter in a way that the guerrillas would understand my position and maybe even sympathize with it. As the start of my argument, I decided, I would quote Carl Schurz and tell them that we had an old saying in the United States: "Our country, right or wrong—when right to be kept right; when wrong to be put right." Just because I had strong feelings against the Indochina war I would not turn my back on my own country and become a propagandist for one of its enemies. I would hope to convince them that my effectiveness was in working as a loyal American, writing the truth and doing my part toward enabling the American people to understand the war. But the depressing probability was that they would not listen to such reasoning.

Mike seemed depressed, too. He knew Asians much better than I and saw discouraging implications for us in their characteristic patience and persistence. They have said they are willing to fight another twenty years if necessary, and Mike was becoming convinced that they were going to keep us prisoner indefinitely, maybe until the war was over. He thought of the end of the first month as a deadline by which we ought to get some word if we were to be freed any time soon. To cheer him up, as well as to give myself a way of appraising our prospects, I worked out a different time frame. I concluded that we should be prepared to wait two months before seeing anything sinister in the delay. The decision, I reasoned, probably would have to be made in Hanoi. We had heard nothing to indicate that our captors were in radio communication with Hanoi. The motorbikes we heard sputtering off along the paths and roads at night and returning before dawn must be the chief means of communication with their next echelon headquarters. It was conceivable that even this regional headquarters had to use couriers to keep in touch with Hanoi; everything we had seen so far was so primitive and mobile and temporary that it seemed reasonable to assume that the stories about elaborate radio antennas were just as exaggerated as the reports of a Communist Pentagon somewhere out here along the Cambodian frontier. Supposing that a courier had to make his way by land all the way to Hanoi, he would have to ride a motorbike or bicycle by night and hide in the daytime. There was heavy fighting in northeastern Cambodia and Southern Laos, so that he probably would have to go on foot through those areas. It could easily take him a month to carry our dossiers to Hanoi. Then, I reasoned, the counterintelligence people there would have to cable to Paris, Moscow, Stockholm, and other world capitals to check the various references we had supplied. Once the information was received and a decision made, the courier would have to make the long trip back to find us again in southeastern Cambodia and deliver the word that we were to be released. Two months seemed a conservative enough estimate.

There were times, however, when I thought of escape. Riding along in the back of the Land Rover among rifles and machine guns or sitting in a grass shack with pistols and rifles left unattended just a few steps away from us, I thought of what it would take to make a successful run for it. We could not count on finding any Cambodian peasants who would be willing to help three strange Americans; from what we had seen, their sympathies appeared to be entirely on the Communist side. That meant that if we had to travel any length of time we would have to carry our own rice and a pot to boil water and build our own fires. Along with some weapons, we would have to grab some canteens, a sack of rice, and one of the cigarette lighters that the guerrillas kept in their pockets.

Another problem would be wild animals. In one of our evening chats, Hai had told us about the poisonous snakes that live in the jungles, with venom so strong that it causes death in five minutes. He had told us how elephants stomp through the countryside. He had given us some instructions—not entirely comforting—as to what to do about tigers: "Beat on the ground with a stick. That makes the tiger roll up in a ball. Then blow a whistle, and he will run away."

A long flight in this strange and hostile region did not seem promising. I decided that the only escape plan with a chance of success was to slip away to a hiding place near an open field or dry rice pasture where we could immediately put out a signal to catch the attention of a plane and hope for a quick pick-up by helicopter. My white shirt and pants were the best materials we had for a signal. I thought we could rip them apart and spread them on the ground to spell the word "HELP" or possibly just "U.S."

But as I considered these plans, I knew that they had little chance of success and would be used only under desperate circumstances or in the distant future. They really weren't much more than daydreams. Besides, there was still plenty for a newspaperman to learn about these revolutionists whose war of independence had been going on for twenty-five years and who now had withstood the might of the United States for eight years with no sign of giving in.

Much of what the guerrillas told us was pretty doctrinaire. A broad-faced young woman joined our little task force for a week or so and sometimes would sit and talk with us. She moved with a smooth grace that gave elegance to her plain blue cotton shirt and black pajama pants. She said she was a nurse, and she advised Mike to eat plenty of a spinach-like vegetable when he complained of a stomach ache. Her soft voice and kindly manner made me think of her at first as a beautiful Asian Florence Nightingale. She was sick herself for a few days and lay most of the time on her straw mat outside our door, her knapsack and gun and kerosene lamp beside her. When she felt better, she apologized for not having come to talk with us for a while, explaining that she had not been well. All this prepared us to feel friendly toward her. But almost everything she said was such hard-line stuff that friendship seemed impossible. For example: "We know that there are good people and bad people in America. The good people will join us to support our revolution. We will trample over the bad people." Remarks like that were conversation stoppers.

With Hai and the others, however, our relationship was becoming less formal and more relaxed. But even Hai kept giving us bits of revolutionary orthodoxy. "If you are good you will meet with goodness because the people will help you and protect you," he would say. "If you are cruel and barbarous you will meet with cruelty and barbarity." And he and the others often told us, in almost exactly the same words, "To live without our freedom and independence is

as good as being dead; to die for the revolution is nothing."

But as he sat around with us in the evenings, cracking
the knuckles of his toes and running his fingers through his
greying brush cut to make the hair stand up straight after a
bath, he went far beyond dogma and began giving us his
own thoughts about the nature of the war. Some of them
were well off the straight Marxist track. For example, he
extended the idea we heard so often from the guerrillas
about there being good and bad Americans to a concept of
good and bad businessmen.

There are three kinds of capitalists in America, he said.
There are those who are definitely making money from the
war, the munitions makers who want the war to go on so
that they can continue to sell their war goods. The second
kind are those who make no war goods and thus do not
profit from the war. The third kind are those who can
make either war goods or ordinary peacetime products.
The first group has always joined with the American military class in giving strong support to the war. The second
group came to oppose the war, because the war is so
expensive that it leaves people little money to buy their
products. The third group has been supporting the war
until recently, but now it is shifting to the opposition
because it sees that the war is causing a general economic
decline in America.

Hai told us little of his own background. Mike asked
him once if he had ever been to Hanoi. He replied that he
had not but showed no inclination to go on and tell us
about himself. Wang, the Chinese student from Phnom
Penh, possibly on instructions from Hai, told us later that

Hai had grown up in a peasant family near Hue and had worked on a rubber plantation. When he was seventeen or eighteen, Wang said, Hai began elementary school and first came into contact with the Viet Minh, the Communist-led underground movement against French colonialism. He joined the movement and had been with it ever since. That was twenty-five years ago.

Whether this account was correct or not, Hai was clearly a thoroughgoing peasant revoluntionary and had devoted his life to the movement. One afternoon, squatting on the floor, he told us: "Of course there are lines of authority in the revolutionary army, but we must all live alike and live together. Only by living like the poor can one understand the revolution. This is no place for a family. I have not seen my wife for many years. We will continue to fight until the Americans are driven out and Vietnam, Cambodia, and Laos have gained their independence. Then if other peoples in the world need help in achieving their independence, we will go and help them."

Vietnamese nationalism was the biggest element in Hai's thinking as expressed in his conversations with us. When he talked about solidarity with other peoples in the world, he spoke of the "oppressed" peoples of Africa, South America, and the Arab world rather than of the Communist countries.

Tu showed the same pride in Vietnamese nationalism, despite his initial pretense that he was Cambodian. Once he told us: "We aren't afraid of any invaders, because of our history. We beat back the Chinese invaders five times, the Mongols once, and the French once."

Remarks like those indicated a welcome frankness. The

guerrillas no longer considered it necessary to stick to the official line employed at Paris and Hanoi that the insurgency in Cambodia was 100 per cent Cambodian. In fact, they began to speak almost patronizing of the Cambodians, saying things like, "They have had no experience with war. I don't know how they could get along if it weren't for our help."

One night, after Hai had finished giving us the highlights of the BBC's Vietnamese language broadcast—new debate in the Senate on the invasion of Cambodia and student demonstrations on several American campuses—he told us unexpectedly that there were three kinds of journalists. "There are the socialists, who support our revolution. There are the capitalist journalists, who work for the Americans and the Thieu-Ky regime. And there are those who work for peace and neutrality. If you are found to be good journalists, we will show you many things about the revolutionary front and you can write about it for your papers. If not, we will not kill you, but you must be reeducated."

It was not a promise of early freedom, but it was ground for optimism. In his third category, the journalists who worked for peace and neutrality, I thought I saw a place for us. Hai's words seemed to offer the first clear opening that we could maintain our own integrity and still be acceptable to the guerrillas.

6
attack I

Friday, May 22, was a day of rest and preparation. Our guerrilla escorts, as we had come to think of them, had never told us ahead of time about our night rides from one house to another. There was just a touch on the toe to awaken us and the quiet order, *"Chuan bi di"* ("Get ready to go"). But that Friday we could sense that we were about to make a major move.

The nurse, recovered from her illness, packed her knapsack and filled her little kerosene lamp and replaced the wick with a tight cap for traveling. Tu, after bringing our morning rice to our little room, crouched across the big room next to the wall with a needle and thread to mend a rip in his blue shirt. "Twitch," the neatest of an extremely neat group of people, spent a good half hour going over his green nylon mosquito net picking off black beatles that had lodged in it during the night. He would stand up, hold it toward the light from the big front door, and find some he had missed on one side, then turn it around and look for more on the other side, his mouth and nose twitching as he concentrated on his work. At last he folded the net into a tight square the size of a book and tucked it into his knapsack, a nylon sack with a loop of webbing leading up from two of the bottom corners. At the top of the loop was a short length of light rope, tied around the webbing with both ends hanging loose. After twisting the mouth of the sack carefully together he folded it over the loop of webbing to form two shoulder straps and tied it in place with the rope-ends. He lifted the thirty-pound knapsack to see that the straps were even and that it hung well. It failed the test the first time, and he unpacked the whole thing— his mosquito net, a neat stack of folded extra shirts, pants, and underwear, a plastic bag containing his lighter and cigarette papers and tobacco, two others containing sugar and mixed salt and pepper, a little folder of personal papers and photographs, and a green plastic sheet big enough for a ground cloth or a tent fly. Methodically, he repacked the sack and tied it again until he was satisfied. One of those compact "Ho Chi Minh knapsacks," as I called them, with its standard issue of equipment, was the one thing I wanted to take home to Washington as a souvenir.

Beth, Mike, and I spent much of the day writing articles or notes on conversations of the last day or two with Hai and the others. Mike has an excellent verbatim memory in both English and Vietnamese, and by working together we could reconstruct exactly their long discussions about the nature of the war and the life of a revolutionary. From time to time we would break off to take a nap on the bamboo floor or play "Twenty Questions" or use some of our precious paper to play Beth's word game, in which one person would think of a five-letter word and the other would try to guess it by naming other five-letter words and being told each time how many letters matched those of the secret word.

The big house seemed to be a sort of way station for the guerrillas. The night we arrived, I had noticed the tall wrinkled man of the house quickly pull a small folded piece of paper from a hiding place inside the mat wall of our room and hand it to one of the guerrillas. I was reminded of the tiny envelopes that Wilfred Burchett had described as the Viet Cong's basic means of communication in his account of travels with the National Liberation Front forces inside South Vietnam and assumed that this paper was a note left for our party.

The bedding spread out along the edge of the floor, the knapsack at the head of each mat, the people lounging about—in fact, everything but the repeating rifles and machine guns leaning against the walls and the occasional boom of a shell or drone of an observation plane—gave the impression of a youth hostel. Three young Vietnamese women visitors, who said they were nurses, added to this impression. They must have arrived before we awoke at dawn and spent the day around the big house, much of the time sitting beside their packs in the middle of the floor in their black pajama pants and fitted blue cotton blouses, chatting and carefully combing their long straight black hair, braiding it, and replacing their silver clips. For a few minutes they talked with us, pleasantly although apparently on instructions; they asked no questions but merely repeated such statements as, "The revolution will continue to victory no matter how long it takes."

Ban Tun, the easygoing Cambodian soldier, seemed to have no duties except to gather firewood and carry an occasional can of water from the well to the kitchen, but he was full of energy and found other things to do. He went inside and gathered leaves from different trees around the house and then spent an hour with the Vietnamese, holding up one leaf at a time while they called out the Cambodian and Vietnamese names for the tree. Later, he went out again, this time carrying a long pole with a small basket fixed to a fork at the end. He used the fork to pick fruit off the trees, letting the fruit fall into the basket. He came back with a few sour little green berries for each of us, and a little paper of salt to cut the sourness. They were not bad, and I felt they would make up a little of our vitamin C deficiency.

A big gecko, a lizard named for the croaking sound it makes, walked upside down along one of the roof beams. Ba, our military chief, who had been dozing on his mat, saw it, grabbed a long bamboo pole, and tried to pry it loose. The gecko's adhesive feet held for a few moments, but the jabbing of the pole was too much, and it fell to the floor. Ba pinned it down with the pole and grabbed it at the back of the head to keep clear of the jaws, which were wide enough to bite a finger. He carried it wriggling to the kitchen for an unexpected addition to the evening's soup.

When darkness came and we had gone out to the well for our bath, the three "nurses," their sleek hair and silver clips shining in the moonlight, their packs on their backs, and AK-47s over their shoulders, walked quietly past the well and out along the path on top of a paddy dike. Returning to the house, we found Ba sitting at the desk, writing in cramped script on a tiny piece of paper by the kerosene flame. We felt we were going to move that night, but we thought it better not to ask. No one volunteered any information.

The call came at 3 A.M. Tu quietly told us the time and said we would be leaving soon. He brought a snack of rice gruel and a dish of salted peanuts. The gruel was hot and reminded Mike of the way Asians can tell whether a person comes from a poor background or not: If he grew up in poverty, he has the habit of running his spoon around the edge of the dish to pick up the part that has begun to cool. A few minutes later, at Tu's whispered order, we slipped out of the house, finding our shoes and sandals laid out as usual at the bottom of the ladder, and walked fifty yards along a moonlit path to the Land Rover, hidden under a neighboring house. We climbed in, finding seats among packs, rifles, a coconut, and a small basket full of chirping chicks. We rode the rest of the night along back roads, with the glare of American phosphorus flares behind us and on both sides and the occasional boom of artillery to remind us that the war was close by.

At dawn, we could see rows of wooden houses on stilts as we drove into a good sized village. The Land Rover stopped in front of a house. We covered our heads with our sarongs as our escorts spoke with a group of Cambodians. When the consultation was over and our accommodations were arranged, Tu beckoned us out and we scam-

pered up a ladder after him into a small room at the left of
the front door. It was separated from the rest of the house
by a row of tall wooden wardrobes. The woman and man
of the house spread out a mat on the slatted floor and
hung blankets on lines to conceal us further, but we could
see brown eyes at every crack as the children of the village
passed the word that some Westerners had come to town.
When I would smile at a glimpse of a child's face it would
quickly drop out of sight and then slowly return to the
crack as curiosity overcame shyness.

The usual thing had been to sleep after a night ride, and,
after a good second breakfast of rice, string beans, beef,
and *nuoc mam*, the fermented fish juice that Vietnamese
use like ketchup, we lay down side by side on the mat. We
were just getting settled, when Tu returned and told us
"*Chuan bi di*" with more urgency than usual. We grabbed
our bags, and he led us down a back ladder. There was
barely time to grab my shoes, let alone put them on, and I
followed him barefoot, running across the back lots to a
dirt road. The drone and whine of planes and the bang-
bang-bang of helicopters began to sound in the distance.
We were part of a mass exodus of villagers and guerrilla
troops, running pell-mell to get out of town ahead of an
attack. The crowd veered off the road and cut diagonally
through a rice paddy a foot deep in water with another six
inches of soft mud underneath. We took high steps as we
splashed through the paddy. Ba and Tu were on ahead,
looking back from time to time to urge us to keep up.
Climbing over a low dike, we came to the next paddy, this
one just deep mud, thick with the tracks and dung of
water buffalo. My muddy pants clung to my legs as I kept

running, with an occasional glance backward to see how
Beth was making it. I wondered how I could ever write a
description of what was happening and still stick to my
line that I am a prudent reporter who never risks getting
into physical danger. Puffing and wheezing a bit by this
time, I overtook two women carrying babies and a soldier
with a live chicken under his arm. Without thinking, I
asked the soldier, "Think there'll be much more of this?"
and when he turned his head at the sound of the strange
language and saw the strange Western face I'd never seen
such a startled look in my life.

Just in time, we reached the edge of the second paddy
and entered open land with brush and occasional trees.
The sound of a patrolling helicopter grew louder. As the
soldiers and villagers ran ahead and fanned out to disperse
and hide from the planes, our little group stopped briefly
while Ba shinnied up a tree for a look behind us. I took the
opportunity to tie my shoelaces together and sling the
shoes through the strap of my flight bag for easier carrying. Ba must have reported that there was still time to run
farther before going into hiding, because we took off
again, running through a tangle of waist-high brush and
vines. After a few minutes of this, Hai struck off in one
direction with Mike and Beth, and Twitch motioned for
me to follow him in another. We came to a clump of low
trees with some freshly-cut branches thrown over the tops
of nearby bushes. Twitch pointed toward a low gap in the
brush and indicated that I should burrow back inside. He
kept waving me farther back until I was well covered with
branches and leaves and then crouched a few feet away,
listening and watching the sky. In the distance we could

hear artillery shells, helicopters, propeller planes, and jet fighter-bombers. He must have heard something else, too— the faint roar of the biggest bombers, which fly so high they rarely can be seen or heard. *"B nam hai"* (B-52) he whispered. He pulled a wad of cotton in half, gave me part of it, and signaled for me to put it in my ears and lie flat on my face with my eyes closed. As I turned over to press my face into some fresh dirt, I noticed that I was squarely on top of an anthill and that there was no place to move because I would brush against a buzzing swarm of bees if I went further back into the burrow. I lay there, expecting the ground to shake and my eardrums to burst if the big bombs fell close. When nothing happened for a few minutes, I peeked at Twitch. He caught my eye and motioned again for me to keep my face down and my eyes shut. I risked another look, and this time I saw him unsnap the leather holster of his pistol. He knew what I must be thinking. He stuck out his finger like a pistol, pointed it at me, and shook his head, then pointed it at the sky and nodded his head. "This is for them, not for you," he was saying. There was a lull in the sounds of the planes, and he passed me his canteen for a drink and then took a small brown paper parcel from his knapsack. He opened it, tore the paper in half, and handed me one of the halves containing five lumps of sugar. Sweets raise the spirits as well as supplying quick energy, and I quickly felt better.

By this time, the sun was high and the day was getting hot. Twitch opened his knapsack again and took out his green plastic sheet, tying two corners to tall bushes to make an awning. He opened the sack again, took out his cigarette makings, tied up the sack, rolled a cigarette, and had a quiet smoke. The continual tying and untying of the knapsack was part of a guerrilla's system of always being ready to go at a moment's notice.

Another emergency, and he snatched down the awning, folded it, and put it into his pack. It was planes again, closer this time. I could hear dive bombing a few miles away, and occasionally there was the scream of a jet almost overhead. The branches were so thick that we could not possibly have been seen. Twitch was so calm, as he peered up through the leaves, that I felt quite safe—a good bit safer than I shall ever feel again riding in a helicopter over a wooded landscape where snipers may be hiding.

The planes went away, but we heard a new sound. The clanking of tank treads and bursts of heavy machine gun fire were coming closer and already seemed not more than a mile or two away. U.S. armor experts had been telling me three weeks earlier that their tanks could race through relatively open country like this at thirty-five miles an hour. I didn't see how we could get out of their way if they happened to be coming toward us. But the sounds began to recede. We were safe.

After a motionless wait, Twitch noiselessly got to his feet and looked through the bush tops in the direction of the departing tanks, moving his head back and forth like a snake as he concentrated on seeing past leaves and branches. Satisfied, he was just getting ready for another smoke, when Ba appeared. They whispered together and then went off through the brush, taking their rifles but leaving their packs and pistols near me. I heard what sounded like chopping or digging and guessed that they were building a bunker. When Twitch returned, I tried to ask him with hand motions if I could help with the job. He rushed off again and returned a few minutes later with instructions for me to pick up my shoes and bag and follow him. He led me a hundred yards through the brush to another grove where Mike and Beth were sitting with Hai. They had hung up some green plastic and cloth sheets that would blend with the foliage and keep the shifting sun off us and had spread other plastic sheets on the ground to keep us off the damp earth. The noises I had heard had been the sound of their chopping branches to fill out gaps in the canopy. Twitch reported to Hai, and Hai told us that Twitch had been worried about me and had misunderstood my sign language. "He said he wanted to take especially good care of you," Hai said. I thought it was nice to be considered of particular importance, probably because the *Post-Dispatch* is such an important newspaper, but Hai went on: "He was worried about you because you are so much older and so much more frightened than the others." I hadn't thought of myself as being any more terrified than anyone else, but I made a mental resolution to put on a better act. My notes of the incident included a reminder to myself: "Must assume attitude of unconcern or even bravery."

Ba and Wang and Ban Tun had been out scouting and returned with the word that the planes had bombed a wooded place several miles away where there were no people at all. They had learned that the tanks had followed a road that ran past us two miles away; their sounds had approached and receded as the road passed its closest point to our hiding place.

Ba went off again, and I hoped he would be returning with a pot of rice and a kettle of hot water. It looked as if we might be spending our first night in the open, but our experience had been that the guerrillas never missed a meal. It seemed likely, too, that we would be doing more walking and less riding if "the other side" had captured our Land Rover. But Ba returned a few minutes later with the word that a messenger from the village had come out to tell us that the Americans had left the village and it was safe to return to the house for dinner. We walked back in the sunset across the rice paddies and along the road into the village, no longer strangers who had to be hidden but veterans of an attack that had threatened us all. Our presence must have been pretty well known by this time. There were some waves and smiles from villagers, and when we reached the house the Cambodian family greeted us warmly. Best of all, dinner was set out on the floor for all of us, the Cambodian family, the guerrillas, and the three captured correspondents, and we sat together in a circle around two big rice pots and side dishes of chicken soup, mashed fish, and peanut paste. The man of the house brought out a bottle of rice wine, poured a big glassful and passed it around for everyone to take a drink of the clear, fiery stuff. A radio was going somewhere, and I heard a Cambodian song that seemed to include the noises of animals. It reminded me of "Old MacDonald Had a Farm," and Mike, Beth, and I sang them a few verses, complete with all "quack-quacks" and "oinks-oinks." It was a friendly and convivial meal, but it ended suddenly when Tu told us the village was not a safe place to spend the night and we would have to take off immediately.

As usual, the Land Rover was at the bottom of the ladder ready to go. We piled into the back and rode away, with a lot of waving and wishes of good luck. We started out along a bumpy country road, alternating through forests and open country and eventually onto a broad plain of flat paddy land. The flooded paddies stretched off into the darkness as far as we could see and reflected distant phosphorus flares. Hai, who had taken several good drinks of rice wine, sat in the back with us and was jollier than usual. His round cheeks shook and his eyes wrinkled at the corners as he laughed over one long story after another. One was about coming back from a drinking party and finding to his astonishment that he had all his clothes on inside out. The other guerrillas were a good audience. Their laughter started him off on another yarn. He told of a battle by National Liberation Front soldiers to capture the capital of Kien Hoa province in South Vietnam, perhaps in the 1968 Tet offensive. They lost the battle, but they made up for their disappointment by inventing ridiculous titles they would be given when they finally won the war—positions like Director of Rice Wine Inspection and Sampling and Minister of Courtship and Marriage.

In the midst of our hilarity, we saw headlights about a mile behind us. Someone was approaching, and there was no way to tell whether it was friend or enemy. Our driver turned off onto a narrow dike road across the paddies. We had gone only a mile or so when there was a jolt and the car lurched to the right and came to rest at a steep angle. Climbing out, we saw that we had hit the broken end of a cement culvert. The two right-hand wheels had slipped off the road leaving the Land Rover resting on its bottom. The four-wheel drive did not help; both right-hand wheels spun free as the driver gunned the engine. It was a dangerous place to be stuck. Now and then we heard a reconnaissance plane. We were afraid the observer would see the stalled car as a silhouette against the bright reflection of the flares in the flooded paddy. The moon had risen and was coming out from behind a bank of clouds, adding still more light to the scene. There was no place to hide and no place to run except the narrow road ahead and back and knee deep water stretching off for miles on each side. The driver, a young South Vietnamese who wore a snap-brim Western-style hat and never wanted anyone else to handle the car, took charge of efforts to get it back on the road. He directed some of the others where to dig with a mattock to make a little side ramp where we might shove the car back up to grade level. When we had tried this several times and always found the back wheel blocked by a remaining section of the cement culvert, he concentrated on trying to pry the section loose with a crowbar. Except when we were needed to help push, we three correspondents sat along the side of the road with our sarongs over our heads to hide our Western faces from a long line of guerrilla soldiers and civilians that began to overtake us.

The nurse, who had taken on the authority of a line officer, alternately directed the traffic past our stalled car and ordered us to keep down and keep covered. Most of the soldiers carried carbines or rifles, and most had small knapsacks like those our escorts carried. Some had larger weapons; I thought I could make out a few mortars and recoilless rifles and possibly some heavy machine guns. Many of the soldiers were wounded, hobbling along on makeshift crutches or, in a few cases, being carried in hammocks slung on a pole carried by two men. We were amazed to see so much traffic within a few miles of a string of American firebases. It made us feel safer to have so much company out there in the unprotected plain. There was a scattering of women among the soldiers, including a strikingly handsome woman with a stylish French-twist hairdo. She was tall and wore a khaki uniform. She happened to reach us just as a family with all its household possessions loaded on a water buffalo cart had stopped, its way blocked by our car. She took charge and ordered the man driving the buffalo to lead the team down into the paddy, around the obstruction, and up onto the road beyond us.

As things turned out, we followed her lead to get our car out. We had been getting nowhere, even after prying loose the culvert section. And, possibly out of pride, our guerrillas had not asked for a push by some of the passing soldiers or a pull from the team of buffalo. Help came unexpectedly in the form of about twenty young men from a village ahead, who had learned of our trouble from the passing soldiers. With the driver gunning the engine, they pushed and pulled until it slid all the way down into the paddy.

Mike jumped into the water and helped. The water was over the floorboards, but the engine kept turning. With the wheels spinning, they shoved the machine slowly through the muddy water parallel to the road. Then the driver turned back toward the dike, and a final heave put the car up out of the paddy and once more on the road. Everyone raised his hands above his head and clapped. The villagers stayed with us, walking ahead and looking for more broken culverts that threatened to shunt us off again. Each time, they climbed down the bank looking for sticks of wood, rocks, and chunks of sod with which they literally rebuilt the damaged road so that we could pass.

We must have lost two hours, and the moon was high overhead by the time we reached the edge of the paddy land and reentered the forest. We drove on for several miles and stopped at a crossroad, where crowds of soldiers were sitting around or sleeping. Tu led us over to a log and told us to sit down and cover our faces so as not to attract attention. Presently, after some whispered talk with the other soldiers, our guerrillas joined us and we set out on foot along the side road. The Land Rover drove off down the main road. Within a few minutes, we saw why it was necessary to walk. Deep trenches had been dug alternately from each side of the road running halfway across, effectively blocking any automobile or truck traffic, although several motorbikes overtook us. I guessed that we were entering one of the liberation army's base areas. More indications came when we had hiked five miles, with an occasional rest stop, and reached a hamlet surrounded by sentries with flashlights. Our escorts spoke with them, and there seemed to be some disagreement over whether we could go farther. Tu led us to a little thatched pavilion, no more than a crude bed with benches around it and a roof overhead, where a half-dozen soldiers were sleeping with their rifles and packs beside them. We were very tired. Mike and Beth lay down on the dusty ground and went right to sleep. I sat on the bench and dozed, throwing a clod now and then to drive away a pig or water buffalo that came toward my colleagues. Tu and Ba and the others had gone on into the hamlet, presumably to arrange for a place for us to stay.

They returned for us after an hour and led us through the hamlet, a scattering of houses that stretched for perhaps a half mile. We passed one group of low thatched huts with a sign in front that must have said "Base Hospital." Nurses and soldiers in bandages and on crutches were going in and out. Eventually we came to a row of wooden houses. While we waited at the front gate, Tu and Ba went forward with Ban Tun to speak with the owner, an older man with greying hair and a lively manner. From his gestures, we judged that he was refusing to let us stay at his place, and only with difficulty did they persuade him to go along with us to try to find room at one of the other houses. We made three other stops, and the old man kept wanting to turn back, before we found a house that would take us in. By that time dawn was breaking and we were so tired from twenty-six hours of travel that we scarcely noticed what the place looked like. We lay down on a mat and slept.

When Tu awakened us for breakfast a few hours later, he explained what the trouble had been: "The people here didn't know us. When they saw we were with three Westerners they would not believe that we were members of the revolutionary front. But we showed them our pictures of Norodom Sihanouk and Ho Chi Minh and were able to convince them. Now they have made us welcome and brought us gifts of food." He couldn't resist drawing a contrast with the other side: "The Thieu-Ky soldiers are not like this. They arrest anyone who does not give them whatever they want."

Hai later gave us some news about the attack of the day before. He said 110 tanks and 3,000 men had taken part in a drive that came to within 200 yards of the house where we had breakfast and later returned to eat dinner. He said it passed within two miles of our hiding place in the woods, but the column as usual kept to the road and thus missed us. He said that American troops went into the village market place and raped one woman. As was so often the case, there was no way to confirm the truth.

7
comrades

When we were first captured, I warned Beth and Mike that there probably would be long periods of idleness, that idleness would lead to boredom, and that we sometimes would get on one another's nerves. The warning may have helped. There were, indeed, some minor annoyances, but these never threatened the faith and respect we developed for one another.

Only the most casual planning had gone into our teaming up for a trip that we thought would last two days at the most. We had not selected each other as companions for weeks, months, or possibly years, much less as comrades on whom we would be depending in matters of life and death. I knew both only slightly. Beth I had met at Cambridge, Massachusetts, several years earlier, when I was there to make a speech about Vietnam and she was preparing to go to Saigon on her first assignment for *The Christian Science Monitor*. I had met Mike the previous winter as one of the founders of Dispatch News Service, the small agency that distributed Seymour Hersh's articles that scooped the rest of the world press repeatedly on the My Lai massacre. Mike asked me not to put too fine a point on his presence in Washington in a piece I was writing about the difficulty of getting the My Lai story published until Hersh took it to the news agency. He explained that he was based in Saigon, writing stories from there for the Dispatch News Service, and avoiding the draft. He had slipped into the United States on a quick visit and wanted to slip out without alerting Selective Service officials.

I had been going to Southeast Asia every year or so since 1960 to keep track of the deepening American intervention there, which I had soon come to consider something very close to imperialism. The reality on the ground was always so different from the official speeches and briefings that much of my writing was devoted to exposing the untold side of the war and showing up the self-delusions by which policy makers fooled themselves as they tried to fool the American people into believing that America's vital interests were at stake, that the war was a pure case of aggression from the north, that the various regimes in Saigon were continually growing stronger, that the National Liberation Front survived through terror alone, and that there always was light at the end of the tunnel.

This time, there were new elements. Nixon had begun a gradual withdrawal of American troops. Political unrest in

South Vietnam was seething, with new groups such as the
disabled war veterans clamoring for reforms and, if necessary, the overthrow of the government of President
Nguyen Van Thieu. Cambodia had abandoned its tradi-
tional neutrality with the ouster of Sihanouk, and major
American intervention there seemed likely despite official
reassurances to the contrary. By coincidence, the brief
American invasion began the day I arrived at Saigon's Tan
Son Nhut Airport after a few days in Bangkok. President
Nixon had just announced it, and an American stranger
told me the news as I waited in line to clear health and
immigration.

It was a perfect time for another look at the war, and
my plan was to spend a week or so each in South Vietnam,
Laos, Thailand, and Cambodia. My managing editor had
told me that this would be my only foreign trip in 1970,
the only time I could be spared from my duties of running
the *Post-Dispatch* Washington Bureau. He had also warned
me against traveling anywhere in Cambodia outside Phnom
Penh, reminding me that nine newsmen had been captured
in the Cambodian countryside.

In Saigon, one of those whom I wanted to see was Mike,
whom I knew to be well acquainted with South Vietnamese politics and an aggressive, independent-minded reporter who probably would have a good understanding of the
real situation in Cambodia. I met him by chance at a press
conference at the An Quang Pagoda one morning after I
had spent several days flying into the new American firebases being blasted out of the jungle in Cambodia and
writing the usual dispatches about the discovery of enemy
caches of weapons and rice. Beth was at the Pagoda, too,

and Mike was good enough to give us a running translation of the monks' charges of repression at the hands of the Thieu-Ky regime.

Mike and I had dinner that evening at the Aterbea, a little French restaurant that has not been ruined by the war. We both felt that the story of the American invasion and its modest results was running a bit thin and that a more significant story was what was happening to the Cambodian people and the Cambodian countryside. He proposed that we drive up Route 1 after the invading South Vietnamese column and see how far we could get toward Phnom Penh. With luck, assuming the column had cleared the entire route, we could drive all the way, stay overnight, and be back the next evening. He suggested that we ask Daniel Southerland of *The Monitor* to go along. We borrowed the International Scout and arranged that Mike would pick me up at six o'clock the next morning. As it turned out, Dan was unavailable but Beth wanted to go in his place. She was on a year's leave of absence from *The Monitor* to work in Vietnam on a grant from the Alicia Patterson Foundation.

That was about all I knew about my two colleagues as we started off together that morning in May. In the weeks that followed, we came to know each other like brothers and sisters.

Beth's worst moment in the entire forty days, she has said since, was the night when Mike and I lay down and went to sleep in the little shack at the base camp instead of sitting up to see if her hunch was right that the guerrillas were going to fix one of their occasional bedtime snacks of tea, leftover rice, and jerked water buffalo; when they

looked around to offer some to the Americans, they saw
that only Beth was awake and didn't bother sharing it.

I found myself growing irritable sometimes, always over
something petty. Once it was over Beth's messiness in
writing the translation of our dossiers into French. Another time it was over my failure to persuade either of
them that there was some merit in working to inspire
esprit de corps among members of a newspaper staff or in
having an editor's blue pencil between the reporter and the
published article. I was annoyed until I realized that our
disagreements reflected the difference between two genera-
tions of reporters, the one still seeking the elusive goal of
some absolute truth and objectivity, the other bent upon
untrammeled self-expression.

With Mike, it was his habit of hunching forward an inch
or two at a time when we were talking with Tu or Hai until
I always wound up peering over Mike's shoulder. That,
too, had a ready explanation: Mike had lost his glasses the
first day, and he was so nearsighted that he had to get
close to watch the speaker's face and lips to make out the
subtleties of the Vietnamese language.

I am sure that I irritated them with my small compul-
sions like not wanting anyone to use too much toothpaste
at one time and trying to persuade Beth that "anything
worth doing is worth doing well." She disagreed strongly,
as a matter of principle, contending that doing anything
neatly was a waste of valuable time that could be spent
better going on to some substantive effort.

But these were isolated incidents. And if Mike ever felt
annoyance toward either of us he never showed it. Although much the youngest, he was in a way the most

mature. He had a solemnity and dignity that resulted partly from his two or three years in the Far East and served us well in guiding us on how to get along with the guerrillas. He once told us that his boyhood friends in the state of Washington told him on a visit home that he had changed greatly and had become much more serious than before. In the long afternoons, with no one else present, Mike told us stories about his boyhood in southern Washington, his years at Dartmouth, and a summer he spent as a lumberjack in the Northwest woods. His stories of the logging camp provided one useful piece of information for our current experience; he said a logger always slit the bottom hems of his pants so they wouldn't catch on a snag and trip him. He spoke often of his wife, Christine, and her parents, a Chinese merchant family in Cholon, the Chinese section of Saigon. Mike and Christine had been married only a few months.

Beth tended to be impersonal in what she said of herself, although she once remarked that, instead of being a prisoner in Cambodia, she might have been Mrs. So-and-so, a housewife in Scarsdale, if she had accepted a proposal of marriage. When I asked if she regretted the decision, she said she didn't and let the matter drop. Beth had spent several months in Czechoslovakia, including the time of the Soviet-bloc invasion, and several weeks in Russia, where she slipped away from a guided tour and was reprimanded by the Soviet police for visiting an artist's studio that turned out to be off limits to American tourists.

I enjoyed having a new audience for a lot of old stories about my year as cabin boy and cook in the merchant marine and told them about my family and our summer place on an island off the coast of Maine.

We all had written exclusively about the war, and much of our conversation was about its various facets. I could give them details of the political downfall of Lyndon Johnson on the war issue and my analysis that Richard Nixon was not really ending American involvement but trying to make the war palatable to the American people, determined, meanwhile, to do whatever was necessary to prevent a Communist victory in South Vietnam. In Saigon, Beth had become the foremost Western expert on the case of Tran Ngoc Chau, the secretary-general of the Lower House, whom President Thieu had stripped of parliamentary immunity and imprisoned on dubious charges of espionage. Mike's all-around reporting of the war had included combat coverage in the battle for Hue, political reporting among the various dissident groups, and such offbeat stories as the United States Army's field tests to determine what combination of socks and boots would best avert "paddy foot," a painful skin disease. He discovered that many soldiers were volunteering to spend several days knee-deep in a rice paddy because the resultant "paddy foot" would keep them out of combat for a while.

All of our personal stories indicated that we attached special value to being resourceful and self-sufficient. Beth told us, with pride in herself as well as her father, that she had persuaded him to let her set out alone across the United States as a young girl on a second-hand motorbike. She also took pride in wearing the cheapest sandals she could find, although when it came to buying a flute she had told her father she wanted the best one that money could buy. Mike recalled that, when he worked in the logging camp to earn enough money to return to Dartmouth, he ate little besides soybean flour as the cheapest form of nourishment he could find.

We often said that we considered ourselves fortunate to have such good company, that we could think of no one we would rather have had as companions in the venture. We sometimes passed the time thinking of persons we would least like having along. My suggestions included Joseph Alsop, on the ground that he would have been so irascible that we probably would have been executed the first day. It did occur to me once that it would be interesting to have with us James McDonnell, chairman of the McDonnell Douglas Corporation, so that we could see how he reacted to being on the receiving end of the bombs and rockets from the warplanes he produces in St. Louis. I tried also to imagine how Walter Lippmann would have handled himself in our situation.

If Mike and Beth and I became comrades, something approaching friendship and comradeship also developed between the three of us and our five guerrilla escorts. Eating together was the catalyst. Not that our guerrillas were very talkative at mealtime—their conversation was mainly urging us to eat a second and third helping of rice—but the change brought us out of isolation, put us on something like an equal basis with them, and accustomed us all to seeing a lot of one another at close range.

The two weeks we spent at the base camp began as a period of rest and quiet after the exertion and anxiety of continual flight climaxed by the attack. The rule of remaining undercover in the daytime applied to us all, so that the reconnaissance planes that sometimes could be heard droning overhead could have spotted only the Cambodian peasants, working in the fields or washing clothes or pounding rice in a crude mill, and some scattered grass-roofed huts. Not all the planes were on reconnaissance missions. Some were courier flights, others were propeller-driven Starfighters on their way to and from military operations in some other part of the country. Sometimes a jet fighter-bomber would scream past, on some mission elsewhere. Even the occasional helicopters appeared to be on business that did not concern our immediate region. The guerrillas paid close attention to all these sounds. When a plane came close, they would peer silently through a crack in the door to try to guess what its movements might mean for future actions. There were many other guerrilla troops in the vicinity. Often we saw long lines of soldiers walking along a trail that led past our hut, always with packs and rifles, sometimes withdrawing after a battle with many of them limping on canes or crutches.

We had no way of knowing where we were. As a rough guess, we had traveled one hundred miles since being captured, but we did not know the direction for sure and suspected that some of our movements had been in circles. We did know that we had not crossed the Mekong River. It was quite possible that we still were inside the twenty-two-mile limit that President Nixon had set on the depth of the American incursion, as he called it. Could we have been taken to the elusive COSVN headquarters that Nixon had hoped to find and destroy? If the Central Office for

South Vietnam, Hanoi's liaison organization with the National Liberation Front of South Vietnam (the correct name for the Viet Cong), actually did have a headquarters in the Cambodian frontier region, we may have found ourselves in the midst of it. But we saw nothing as permanent or elaborate as the installation Nixon had described. The hospital, the troops' billets, the several houses where we stayed, all seemed to be peasant huts, borrowed for the time being by the guerrillas. Everything appeared to be as makeshift as the cuts that blocked the road by which we entered the area.

Our moves before we finally got settled at the base camp were makeshift, too. Just before dawn of the second day, we had been awakened and led a mile or so along back paths. Our guide was a small boy of about ten. We reached a hut where we were shown into a dusty storeroom, the walls lined with sacks of rice, and the palm-leaf siding and the thatch of the roof grey with age and hung with spider webs. The only thing clean was a new straw mat that had been unrolled for us on the floor. We lay down but had hardly gotten settled when we were aroused for another short walk to two houses that stood a few yards apart. Tu ordered us to climb up a crotched stick that served as a ladder into the smaller of the two huts, where we three were assigned to one side and the guerrillas to the other.

The main room was about twelve by fourteen feet, with palm-leaf walls and thatched roof supported by a frame of poles cut from small trees. The floor slats were irregular strips of hand-sawn teak. We had entered through the open back door by way of a small porch with a floor made of

branches that provided space for two or three water jars
and three stones on a bed of ashes that formed the family
cookstove. The smoke filtered out through a gap under the
eaves. Across the main room was the front entrance with a
crude door of flat, hand-sawn boards that could be slid
back and forth to open or shut it.

As usual, there was privacy for us to the extent we
wanted it. The guerrillas already had rigged a piece of rope
from front to back and hung a light blanket on it to give us
a separate room; but it had been pushed aside and remained that way most of the time. The thing to do after
an early morning arrival is to lie down and get a little more
sleep, and the guerrillas unrolled their mats and lay down
on their side of the room. We had a new straw mat with a
red mat of woven plastic material on top of it. I moved the
red one so that we could have it under our legs to block
the draft that came up between the slats. It was a poor
house, and there were not enough pillows to go around; I
laid my head on my flight bag. As I looked up at the roof,
I could see that this hut, although not as old as the last
place, was showing the signs of age. Spider webs clung to
the thatch, and black spiders were busy making new ones.
Little tan geckos clung motionless upside down on the
roof poles and then darted a few quick steps. Occasionally
one of them would emit a tiny spurt of excrement. A field
mouse darted out of a burrow in the thatch and ran along
a pole under the eaves toward the kitchen.

Two newcomers were among the guerrillas across from
us. One was a handsome, sullen-faced young Cambodian,
who stretched himself until the joints in his back or
shoulders made a cracking sound. He scowled and mo-

tioned for us to put the red mat back where it belonged, on top of the straw mat. It was his house, and he didn't want any Western intruders rearranging the furniture. It occurred to me that we had been walking and sitting on what was probably his bed and that the red mat had been placed on top to protect it. But even though his annoyance might be justified, I became alarmed. What if he told the guerrillas some false story about us? What if he planted one of their ammunition clips in one of our pockets when we were outside bathing? Mike watched him carefully and concluded from his manner and a redness of his eyeballs that his problem was too much rice wine rather than feet on the bed. Nonetheless, I took the precaution of taking my pants outside with me for a night or two.

The second stranger was the small boy who had guided us across the fields. He brought tea and ran errands and between times wrestled playfully with the men or practiced aiming one of their heavy rifles at the ceiling. The nurse said that he was being kept there for safety's sake and to attend a guerrilla school while his parents were out fighting.

The monsoon rains were approaching. When we had a heavy downpour one evening and the frogs began to croak, Ba and Ban Tun, the Cambodian guerrilla, stripped to their underwear, put on plastic ponchos, and went outside with a pair of long pointed bamboo poles to spear frogs in the moonlight. They came back with a dozen big ones, and soon we were eating a mess of barbecued frogs' legs and dropping the bones through the slats to the chickens underneath. The rain that brought out the frogs was a piece of luck, because our guerrillas had nearly run out of rice and had apologized that we would have to be on short rations until they got more. Hai enjoyed seeing our appreciation of the delicacy and said, "In the liberated zone, if you don't get one thing you get something else, so you don't starve."

There were two big sacks of rice next to our mat; but these belonged to the Cambodian family, and the guerrillas did not touch them. The next day they obtained a small sack for themselves—they said they were given rice by the Cambodians but bought meat, vegetables, seasonings, and other supplies—and spent an hour carefully refilling the long salami-shaped cloth tubes in which they carry it across their shoulders when marching.

One afternoon the guerrillas began talking excitedly among themselves, and Mike overheard enough to guess that we were having dog for dinner. Wang told us about it, and said it had been six months since he had had a dog feast. He said they had been able to buy the dog, a white, short-haired animal something like a fox terrier. Hai took out a bottle and a hypodermic needle attached to a rubber tube and seemed to be planning to bleed it to death. We could hear the dog squealing, somewhere out of sight under the house, and then suddenly there was silence. Despite some apprehension on our part, it was quite tasty. There were bits of braised dog meat served with the rice, some tiny bite-sized dog steaks served separately, a bowl of dog bouillon, and afterwards a few barbecued dog spareribs each. The meat was dark and rather strong, something like venison.

The guerrillas were surprised to learn that Americans don't eat dog. When Mike explained that in the United

States a dog often is considered a member of the family, they found that hilarious. We decided not to test their credulity by telling them that American dogs have special food, sometimes wear coats, and are taken to special hospitals when they get sick.

It was a mark of the relaxed atmosphere of our little task force that we could laugh together. One night, partly for our benefit I supposed, Ban Tun began chanting some Buddhist prayers he had learned in his childhood. Hai, looking more than ever like an oriental Santa Claus with his chubby cheeks and twinkling eyes, began dancing around the chanting Cambodian, who by this time was sitting cross-legged, his shoulders draped with a blanket. Even sad-eyed Tu caught the spirit and balanced three pillows on the chanting Buddha's head.

When they had had enough of that horseplay, Tu asked us to sing a song. We started "We Shall Overcome," thinking that would appeal to them, but Tu interrupted and seemed to be asking for some particular song. Mike listened carefully and said, "I think he's asking us to sing 'the song about the animals.' " He wanted an encore of "Old MacDonald Had a Farm," and we delighted them by singing all the verses we could think of.

Another laugh was at Wang's expense. The twenty-six-year-old son of a wealthy merchant in Phnom Penh was the dude of the task force. They all took two or three baths a day, but he took four or five. Around the house, he wore a spotless white sportshirt and khaki shorts. Several times a day he combed his wavy black hair and clipped off the few hairs of his sparse beard with a cheap fingernail clipper he kept chained to his Zippo cigarette lighter. One morning when two of the others came back from a motorbike trip, they reported that some of the older women in the neighborhood had been asking a lot of questions about Wang. They wanted to know how old he was, where he came from, and above all whether he was married and might be available as a match for one of their unmarried daughters. When he showed embarrassment they increased their ribbing, and we had the experience of seeing a guerrilla blush.

As we got to know him, Wang told us that he had joined the revolution two years earlier, "When Lon Nol began to get power and it became difficult for Chinese students to go to China for their education." He spoke four Chinese dialects, Vietnamese, Cambodian, and a few words of French and English. He received an allowance of about one dollar a month from his parents and used much of it to buy cigarettes for the others and extra meat and special treats such as an occasional package of twisted sweet rolls that look and taste much like New England crullers. Once when our writing paper was almost exhausted and the last of our ballpoint pens had given out, he came back from town with a thick school notebook with a picture of Sihanouk on the front and two brand new Bic pens for us. We learned that it was he who had bought our sarongs and toilet articles the second day.

Several times we offered to pay for our own food while we remained captives or, as we put it, until they had finished checking our credentials, but they said that wouldn't be necessary unless we wanted some special foods. As long as we ate what they ate, they were getting an additional food allowance of one piaster per man per day that would cover our expenses.

We didn't have our money, of course—except for $200 in U.S. twenty-dollar bills that I carried zipped in my money belt and had decided not to mention when we were ordered to empty our pockets the first day. The money we had carried in our pockets had presumably been kept with our cameras and other belongings that were taken from us the first day. Hai told us he hoped we would get the things back and asked us each to write a detailed inventory of what had been taken, including amounts of money, descriptions of our cameras, and a list of all our credentials. My list included my reporter's notebook, a book about Cambodia, and a mimeographed report on alleged defoliation flights by American planes over the Cambodian frontier region, something I had hoped to check out in the course of the assignment. Beth's list included Mary Baker Eddy's *Science and Health*.

Mike's reddish hair was getting very long, and one afternoon Hai asked if he would like a haircut. Tu took out a pair of clippers and a comb and pair of scissors and went to work with the flair of a professional, first trimming and then thinning the thick hair. Hai watched carefully and had one criticism. "Shave off the sideburns," he ordered. Mike expressed no view, but Tu seemed to want to leave them the way they were, down to the earlobes, even though none of the guerrillas wore sideburns. After some discussion of the esthetics of the case, they compromised and Tu used a bare double-edged razor to shave off the lower half on each side.

The nightly talks with Hai continued. He would listen to the BBC's Vietnamese language broadcast and then give us the highlights. One night it was a report that twenty-one governments had now recognized the Sihanouk government-in-exile. He said that six of Lon Nol's thirty battalions already had defected to the guerrilla side and that the others sat in their barracks and were not fighting. "And this is not propaganda," he said. "This is the BBC." He was not afraid to admit that Radio Hanoi and the clandestine radio were sometimes unreliable.

Part of what he said was intended to keep us from worrying about our safety. "There are many planes that pass overhead," he said, "but most of them are on special missions. They don't see much, and when they do see something it takes them a long time to turn around." He had a word of instruction: "That run into the countryside was a very common thing with us. Whenever we have to run, just follow us."

"Did you hear the B-52 attacks that afternoon?" he went on. "Nobody was there. Our people know the attack was coming, and they all left. There are four purposes of a B-52 raid: to prepare the way for a military advance, to strike a liberated area that cannot be reached on the ground, to drive the people out of an area, or to drive the people into the cities, where they can be controlled. It is the ordinary people who suffer from the B-52 attacks, not the soldiers of the revolution."

Communist radio broadcasts sometimes carried a theme that often figured in the guerrillas' conversations with us—that American and South Vietnamese air power did not mean a decisive advantage. The guerrillas spoke continually about the vulnerability of the planes and the ease with which the soldiers on the ground could escape air attack, even the supposedly dreaded B-52 raids. One night when their transistor radio was tuned to one of the Communist broadcasts in Vietnamese, we heard a gay little folk song sung by a chorus of boys and girls. From time to time, we could hear the phrase *B nam hai*—B-52—and Mike made out enough of the other words to know that the happy refrain could be translated roughly as, "Who's afraid of the big bad B-52?"

Hai invited us to ask questions, and I asked what would happen to the Roman Catholics in South Vietnam when the revolution was successful, meaning if the Communist side won. I told him that the prospect of a bloodbath had been raised by President Nixon and that this troubled many Americans who might otherwise favor complete American withdrawal. Hai responded by telling us that there was no reason to kill anyone except a few war criminals, certainly not the Roman Catholics. "Religious people have the same objective as the revolutionists," he said. "Unlike the imperialists, we all want to help the people and give them a better life. But the man of the pagoda hopes to accomplish this through philosophy and prayer, while the revolutionist relies on organization and struggle."

We asked if many monks had joined the revolution in Cambodia. "Some monks have put aside the saffron robes for the black uniform of the revolution," he said, "but we don't want all of them yet, because a revolution takes a long time and society must have a balance."

We asked if a person could keep his religious beliefs

after joining the revolution. "There is no contradiction at all between religion and revolution," he replied. "You can have religion, too, if you want to. Both have the same purpose, bringing benefit to the people. Only when religion lets itself be used by foreigners and reactionaries to oppose the revolution does the revolution oppose it. For example, many Catholic leaders in Saigon have let themselves be used in this way. But it is certain that the common people who are religious, once they understand what the revolution is about, can't help but support it."

Life in the little hut settled into such a fixed routine that we began to wonder if this had been the goal of our travels and if we were going to be held there indefinitely. But Hai reminded us that everything is temporary in the world of the guerrilla. "We will not move tonight unless circumstances change," he said. And then he suggested that a major change would come before long in any case: "The rainy season will begin soon. Then there will be few foreigners or government people who will remain with our troops, because the troops will go out of the houses and live in the forest and our offensive will begin." I took it that "foreigners" included us and that "government people" included himself, since he seemed to be a political agent of some importance.

There had been no advance word when Tu touched me on the toe early one morning and said, "*Chuan bi di*." We had learned to keep our few extra clothes and toilet articles packed, so there was no problem in slipping out the front door and down the ladder in the dim light of early dawn. Tu instructed us to cover our heads with our sarongs, to avoid spreading the knowledge that three Westerners were in the area. He and Ban Tun led us out past the well where we had bathed every night and the field beyond where we had squatted for a makeshift toilet. After crossing a broad open field, we turned into a small forest, proceeding once more along a rutted forest road, and then turned abruptly into a narrow trail that wound in among the trees, underbrush, and tangled vines. We had gone no more than a half-mile altogether, when we came to a wide place that had been cleared by cutting down saplings. A heavy canopy of branches and vines blocked the sky completely. Ban Tun unrolled the straw mat he had been carrying, and Tu told us we could sit down and rest. Ba approached from another direction, and the three guerrillas set down their packs and rifles, slung their nylon hammocks between trees, and settled down for a long wait. We guessed that they either expected an attack or else wanted us not to see something that would be going on that day back at the house.

Hai and Wang brought breakfast from the house—hot rice and tea—and then took away the pots and dishes, leaving the rest of us once more to ourselves.

The Cambodian, who seemed lonely because he had no one but Wang and Ba to talk to, came over and sat with us. He first used his sheath knife to help us cut out some snags underneath the mat. Then he took out his ball-point and showed us how to play Cambodian ticktacktoe. It is played with the same crosses and circles as the American game, but the object is to get five in a row instead of three. Each player tries to get five marks in a vertical, horizontal, or diagonal line and tries at the same time to block the other's attempts to do the same thing first. We played on

the squares of the woven mat, and each game spread out
irregularly until one side won.

When that palled, I thought of a project I'd had in mind
many years for such an occasion: I would make a chess set.
Using my pocket knife, which the guerrillas had returned
to me with my toilet articles, I first cut a pair of castles
from a small tree branch to try out one of the simplest
men first. Then I chose one of the most difficult and
carved a passable knight. Mike found a larger branch and
carved an excellent queen, and I made a good king with
the usual cross on top. We stripped the bark from the
white men and left it on for the blacks. Beth took responsibility for the pawns and made all sixteen of them by
cutting bullet-shaped pegs from thin branches. She did
very well after I rejected the first one as not good enough.
It looked as if we would not finish the project that day, so
we cut off several branches of different sizes for the rest of
the set.

This was just in time. It began to rain. Ba, Tu and Ban
Tun folded and packed their hammocks while we packed
the chess materials and rolled up the mat. Tu led us farther
into the forest until we came to a small open hut made of
logs and grass. It was no more than a roof and floor, the
floor made of branches and supported by stilts three feet
above the ground. Five big sacks of unhulled rice took up
more than half the space, but we crowded into what was
left to get out of the rain. Presently the shower passed, and
Hai and Wang came with supper, this time some chicken
and vegetables in addition to the tea and rice. After the
meal, we waited until nearly dark and then started back to
the house. It was raining again, so Mike and I took off our

pants and shirts and packed them in our bags to keep them dry.

Walking back in our sarongs, we had an indication of Hai's importance in the guerrilla movement. A Vietnamese guerrilla saw our single-file procession of eight strangers and challenged Ban Tun, who was in the lead. Hai stepped forward and spoke briefly with the man. He let us continue on our way. Hai told us, "If I hadn't been along, you would all have been arrested. "

Back at the house, Mike was able to eavesdrop enough to learn why we had been taken to the woods. After asking how we had spent the day, Hai told the others it was too bad they had gone to all the trouble to take us into the woods, since we hadn't urinated any oftener than the two trips a day permitted when we were staying in the house. It had been simply an attempt to make life more convenient for us, but our fluid intake was so low that twice a day was enough.

Hai took out his sheath knife and helped us finish the chess men. He seemed fascinated with the project, and it turned out he also was anxious to play. As we finished, the Cambodian man of the house, in an unexpected show of friendliness, brought a square board and a piece of chalk and drew the sixty-four squares for the game.

Tu and Mike played the first game, with Hai and me kibitzing. They caught on quickly, since they already knew a Chinese version of the game called elephant chess, which has some different moves and additional men including elephants and artillery pieces. They were intensely competitive and excited over each move. I began to fear that the game would take on East-West symbolism and become overly committed. But they were good losers and enjoyed the game for itself. When it was over, Mike asked if they would like to play another. "No," said Hai. *"Dang, dang; ngu, ngu"* ("fight, fight; sleep, sleep"), and he unrolled his mat and lay down for a nap.

After another defeat, Hai made a typically Vietnamese remark that defied any precise interpretation: "We can't lose yet because we have never won from you. We're just like Nixon in Southeast Asia. He can't lose because he has never defeated us."

They played chess the way they fought. The moves were fast, with rarely more than ten or fifteen seconds taken to study the possibilities. They were too polite to tell us to hurry, but when Hai and Tu were playing each other Hai once said after roughly a half minute, "Are you going to play or should we take naps?" They could lose a rook or queen without showing any dismay and then rush on to try to win with what was left. They could size up a situation so quickly that if Mike or Beth or I made a careless move and put our queen in check Hai or Tu would capture it in a flash before we had a chance to see the trouble, let alone ask to make the move over. I kept the chess men tied in one of my handkerchiefs, and Tu and Hai asked me after every meal to take them out for another game. When we heard a plane they could hardly drag themselves from the game but waited until the sound was almost overhead before going to the crack in the door for a look.

Beth, who had learned to play with her father, had a peculiar game that enabled her to beat the Vietnamese often. She would open fast, using her queen on the offensive, often forcing or quickly accepting an exchange of major pieces early in the game. Their own impulsiveness kept them from taking full advantage of the weakness of such an opening. We wondered how they would react to being beaten repeatedly by a woman, but they seemed entirely lacking in male chauvinism.

Along with the pleasure of playing chess, we had a new variation in our diet, provided as usual by Ban Tun. He had struck up an acquaintance with a woman who was working in a cornfield near the first place where we hid in the forest. He went back to see her and returned with a brown paper package. He opened it furtively and carefully showed the others that it contained black strips of jerked water buffalo. He wrapped it again, and they hung a blanket across the back door and looked out to see that no one was coming before Hai began stewing some of the smoked meat and barbecueing the rest in preparation for dinner. As we sat down to eat, he explained the secrecy: The Cambodian who owned the house disapproved of eating water buffalo and would be offended if he found us eating it in his home. Many Cambodians feel the same, we were told, on the ground that the water buffalo is essential as a draft animal. When the owner walked in in the midst of the meal, they covered the bowl and said nothing about its contents.

Another treat was porcupine, which one of the peasants caught and sold to the guerrillas. Still another was a fresh pineapple that Hai methodically skinned and cut into a thick, juicy slab for each of us one hot afternoon. We ate it their way, dipped in coarse salt to cut the sweetness.

Games and food and some interesting talk made the

time pass pleasantly, but we felt a lurking anxiety that we
might be held captive indefinitely. So it was a relief to
begin getting hints that we might possibly be freed before
long. The first was that unexplained remark by Hai about
"foreigners" no longer being able to stay with the soldiers
of the Cambodian front when the rainy season began.
Another time, Hai gave us something of a pep talk about
the writing we would be able to do after living with them
for a time. "You can write articles or perhaps a book of
great historical significance," he said. "You could write
about the successful war of one small nation against the
United States. It would be read around the world, especially by other small nations that want to oppose the United
States and don't know how."

Once he asked us abruptly how long we would like to
stay with them if we could have our preference. "You
must understand," he said, "that it has not yet been
decided whether or not you truly are news correspondents,
but I am asking your wishes if the question should be
determined in your favor." Mike replied in Vietnamese
before translating the question and his answer for Beth and
me. He said we would like to stay another month.

That was all right with me and with Beth. Adopting the
gravity that goes with age in the orient, I made a little
speech, waiting for Mike to translate it a sentence at a
time: "Except for one circumstance, we are perfectly
happy to be here with you. That one thing is the anxiety
on the part of our families because they do not know
whether we are alive or dead. If only we could have some
word from them that they know we are alive and well we
would feel quite at ease. This is a wonderful opportunity

for a journalist, to be able to observe the other side of the war. As soon as your investigation is completed and you have determined that we are 'good people,' we hope that we can be given freedom of movement and be permitted to talk more with people and inspect areas where the fighting has taken place. Another month would be just the right amount of time, because that would take us just past the end of June, when President Nixon has promised that all American troops will be withdrawn."

Hai listened carefully, paused a moment, and said, "That's a good answer." That was the end of the conversation.

8
attack II

June 9 began inauspiciously, with no hint that it would be one of the most dangerous and significant days of our lives. The early monsoon rains that had kept us inside the house had let up, and Hai said he was going to send us out into the forest again. The first full month of our captivity had passed two days earlier, with no firm indication whether we would be released soon or held for the duration of the war, either to be "reeducated" or in accordance with some scheme to enlist us gradually into serving the revolutionary organization as captive writers.

Ba and Ban Tun led us out across the fields in the dawn. No one else was stirring. We skirted puddles left from yesterday's rain and, entering the woods, walked carefully to avoid hanging vines and sharp snags where ground had been cleared for the small cornfield. We headed straight for the little thatched shed where the sacks of rice were

121

stored. We were left to ourselves. Ba slung his hammock between two trees, and Ban Tun lay down in the lean-to for a pre-breakfast nap. Now that we knew the purpose of a day in the forest, that it really was for our own comfort and diversion, we took advantage of the limited freedom. After we had hung up our shirts and underwear, still damp from being washed the night before, Mike picked out a straight twig and carved himself a pair of chopsticks. He and Beth walked a few yards in opposite directions along the trail and practiced their bend-downs and stationary running. I tramped around the area in search of long, flexible vines for several projects I had in mind. One was a makeshift belt for Beth. We all had been losing weight, and her fitted pants were beginning to hang low around her hips. We worked a vine through the hem and tied the ends together to take up the slack and hold the pants at the proper level. To my satisfaction, I found that I could still weave a Turk's head knot, the way I had done in the Boy Scouts forty years earlier, and have a ring to hold my sarong in place around my neck. Finally, the zipper on my flight bag had broken, and I needed another vine to keep the bag from falling open.

Ban Tun joined us after breakfast, demonstrating more of his skill as a woodsman. He scanned the ground and then stopped and dug out a big locust that he had spotted by its tiny air hole. He put it into his shirt pocket to be saved for dinner. After catching a few more, he went off with his rifle to try to shoot some doves, and we were left again to pass the time together. We talked poetry, American and Chinese history, and then that old standby, what we would like for our first meal when we got back to

Saigon. (Mike was set on yogurt and dried apricots.) Mike began a desultory lesson in Vietnamese, and then Beth drilled him for a while in French. By noon it had lapsed into a rather boring day.

Suddenly, we heard helicopters in the distance. At the first sound, Ba quickly took down his hammock and packed it, and Beth grabbed our washing off the eaves and bushes. Ban Tun crouched behind a big tree with his pack and his carbine. The three of us sat in the hut, leaning up against the rice sacks with our knees pulled up under our chins. Ba told us to stay out of sight and, whatever happened, not to run.

The branches above were too thick for us to see more than a few glimpses of the sky, but we could hear the pounding of the helicopter engines. They sounded almost directly overhead. Ba grabbed his M-16 rifle and sprinted off through the woods in the opposite direction from our hamlet. Ban Tun waited a moment until the helicopters veered away briefly and then ordered us to hide under the hut. I picked up our bags and shoes and sandals, and we joined the Cambodian soldier on our hands and knees on the cool moist dirt in the three-foot crawl space directly under the rice sacks.

It was frightening. Mike had told Beth and me several times that the helicopters were the worst. Jets and propeller planes flew too high and turned too slowly to be able to spot and hit individuals on the ground. Tanks could move fast, but they usually stuck to the roads, or else one could run to the side and have a good chance of avoiding them. But helicopters, he had said, could chase a man on the ground like a cat chasing a mouse and cut him down with machine gun fire. Now he whispered that our best chance was that the men in the helicopters would not be able to see the square lines on the lean-to roof through the branches. The sacks of rice probably would stop machine gun bullets, he said, but rockets would go right through them. The helicopters returned, and we could hear them circling and diving, so loud that much of the time they must have been just above us. We heard at least one burst of machine gun fire and guessed that it was "reconnaissance by fire," the technique of shooting at random to try to make guerrillas on the ground give away their position by shooting back. After forty-five minutes the helicopters shifted their operations a few hundred yards, and after another ten or fifteen minutes they pounded away into the distance.

Ba returned, picked up his pack, and told us to get ready to move. "Bring your bags," he said. "We are going to another place. This is too good a target." Ban Tun led the way along an overgrown path through the woods, while Ba struck off in another direction. We walked a quarter-mile or so, stepping over tangles of vines and fending branches away from our faces, until we reached a dark, cave-like hollow under a bushy tree, where brush had been spread across the lower branches to make a dense protective cover. For a half-hour the four of us sat silent and motionless, on the chance that the planes would return or the air raid would be followed by a ground attack.

There was another half-hour wait while Ban Tun scouted the area. He came back with a handful of his little sour wild oranges, and we passed the time trying to eat them.

The pulp was so bitter and sticky that it tasted like a mouthful of lemon-flavored pitch.

Finally Ba returned, smiling and confident, and still as starched and natty looking as ever. He leaned his rifle against a log, took off his khaki-colored pith helmet, sat on his haunches, and began a report of what had been happening. Brushing aside the leaves and twigs to make a bare spot on the dirt, he used a stick to scratch a rough map. An X marked the position of the lean-to, and a circle that passed near the X showed the flight pattern of the helicopters during the forty-five minutes they were overhead.

"They were American helicopters," he said. "One was only fifty feet above the treetops, looking for a target. It was so low that the wind from the propeller blades made the trees sway and could have shown the outlines of the hut. I could see the men and their machine guns in the lowest helicopter. There was a Cobra gunship flying higher, and still higher there were two other helicopters."

Scratching another line that curved around to the other side of the attack zone, Ba said that was where he had run when the planes began zooming near the hut.

"I showed myself and fired three shots at the lowest helicopter," he said. "That made them think that some of our soldiers were over there and diverted their attention from the hut where you were hiding. They began circling that spot to try to attack us. But I ran back into the woods and came back to the hut."

He paused a moment. "This is an inferior weapon," he said, slapping the captured American M-16. "I would have hit that helicopter if I had been using an AK-47."

Ba said the Chinese repeating rifle could bring down a

plane from an altitude of more than five hundred meters. He said he had shot down a helicopter a few days before we were captured and named four other planes, including the F-4 Phantom fighter-bomber, that he said he had brought down with the Chinese rifle.

Then he said: "The worst thing you could have done during that attack would have been to run into the open and show yourselves to the Americans. I carry this pistol on my hip, and if that had happened I would have had to shoot you. But I knew that you would not do that. I don't say very much, but I have been observing you carefully. I know that you are good people."

For the first time, he told us something about himself. He had fought against the French in Vietnam, apparently in the southern Mekong Delta region, for many years until the negotiated Geneva settlement brought a temporary peace. Then he settled in Phnom Penh, went to school, and became a star soccer player, a member of Cambodia's team in an international soccer league. He said he once wrote a book about soccer. But the revolution began again, and he went back to the life of a guerrilla in 1960 and had been at it ever since.

Mike asked Ba how long it took to train a man until he was a competent guerrilla soldier. "One year," Ba replied, "long enough to find out if he has the will to endure the battles and the hard life."

The relaxed atmosphere after the danger of the attack seemed appropriate for asking a question that had been intriguing us since almost the first day. "How do you like this assignment?" we asked him. He gave a frank answer: "You remember those battles, when we have run away from the air attacks and the advancing enemy. If I were not with you, I would have been in all of those fights, standing fast and shooting until the last moment. I would have been among the last to run." He said he had been wounded three times and showed us scars on his legs and back to prove it, but he took pride in never having been out of action more than a month. He was a guerrilla by choice, and he liked it.

We had never felt so close. We returned together to the lean-to to wait for nightfall, when we could safely go back to the house for dinner. In the meantime, Wang brought out the teakettle full of boiled water; there were no cups, so he suggested we turn the cover upside down and drink from that.

Now that we had measured up to Ba's estimate of us, he came forth with several things he had been holding back. "Do you remember on the day you were arrested, when you were sitting tied and blindfolded and someone came and spoke with you and loosened your ropes and said that you would not be shot and that if you were truly journalists you would be freed?" he asked. He told Mike: "Well, I was the one who came and loosened your ropes. You asked if I was a captain, and I told you I was only a lieutenant. That was just something to say." Without telling his true rank, he implied that it was a good bit higher than that.

"That was a very dangerous situation for you," he said. "The people wanted to kill you." He used the phrase *"danh chet"* ("beat you to death"). "And some wanted to harm Madame"—indicating Beth. "I left two soldiers with you and went over and assigned another soldier to stay with her. It would not have been right for them to kill you, not knowing whether you were good people or bad people."

(His implication was that it would have been all right to kill us if we had been "bad people.") "The Cambodians are very new at this and have not been part of the revolution for a long time, so they do some things that are not good."

Ba went on with his story of that first day: "That evening, when you talked with the big man—do you remember him?—and he told you that Anh Ba would take care of you? That was I. He told me that was my responsibility. No matter what happened, I was to protect your security. This has been my chief concern these weeks that we have been together. I want you to live. I want to see you safely back with your families. I just want them to see you face-to-face again."

Then came more instructions, and he returned to something he had said earlier: "No matter what happens, don't run or call the Americans. Sooner or later you will be released. If you showed yourselves, it would only make trouble for us. I have a pistol here at my waist. If I had to, in a dangerous situation, I could shoot you. But no matter what happens, I would not do that."

Mike told him that we trusted his judgment completely in getting us out of this situation alive and never would try to run away. I felt that Ba knew this was the truth and that he understood that the question of whether or not to shoot us would never arise.

"I understand," he said. "Living together for a time, one can come to know about another person. I don't usually talk much, but I know these things."

There was another pause. Then Ba decided to go a step further. He spoke in Vietnamese.

Mike turned to Beth and me, his thin face reflecting anxiety mingled with excitement. "I don't know whether I should try to to translate this or not," he said. "I might be wrong. But what I think he said is, 'Although no one has told you yet, you have been judged to be bona fide journalists and you are going to be released.'"

By then it was nearly dark. We walked back out of the forest and through the fields in a light rain, with our sarongs covering our heads. As we neared the well, we could see several figures, villagers taking their evening bath. Ban Tun motioned for us to crouch next to a row of low trees while we waited for them to leave. Beth had followed a few paces behind. I looked around as she swept up to the hiding place, peering out from under the folds of her sarong through her horn-rimmed harlequin glasses, and went down to her haunches. The relief at the prospect of freedom had begun to sink in, and she suddenly was tickled at the way we looked in our strange headdresses. She whispered: "I never felt so much like a character in a grade-B movie."

Hai was waiting for us by the light of a kerosene lamp when we climbed the ladder into the little house. Wang had been to the village on a shopping trip. Hai gave us some soap and said, "You may take your bath, but you must hurry, because we will be moving tonight. But first you will have a visit from a person in higher authority."

At dinner, we all were hungry after the exertion and tension of a long and dangerous day. We each ate three plates full of rice. There was no need for Ban Tun's admonition to eat well, but he wanted to make sure we were fortified for the trip ahead.

We washed our dishes on the little back porch and returned to the main room. Mike and I put on our shirts and combed our hair. We sat and waited.

9
cleared

"The man from higher up is here to see you," Tu told us. "He will come inside in a few minutes."

Ba squatted beside us. "We will be starting on a long march as soon as your visitor has finished talking with you." We exchanged smiles with him over our secret. There was no need for him to tell us to be discreet.

There were footsteps on the ladder at the front door, and a familiar face appeared over the doorsill, the big mouth formed into a broad smile. It was the big man of the first night, the high-ranking North Vietnamese officer who had told us how our case would be handled and had put Ba in charge of our security. Tonight, instead of a khaki uniform, he wore a peasant's black pajamas. He was barefoot, having left his sandals at the bottom of the ladder. He carried a flashlight.

"Do you remember me?" he asked. It was a joking

question. We shook hands warmly like old friends. Although we had seen him only once before, we had often thought and spoken of him as our best chance of survival and eventual release. He was our link with Hanoi, where we felt the leaders must know that it would be in their own best interest to release any bona fide news correspondent. Beyond that, his easy smile and self-confident manner inspired confidence. He must have been an excellent commander.

He introduced his aide, a sharp-featured, slightly shorter man with close-cropped black hair and a red bandana tied jauntily around his neck. Tu brought the teapot and cups and withdrew, and the five of us sipped tea for a moment as we sat cross-legged facing each other, our faces half in shadow and half in light from the single flame of a kerosene lamp set on one of the rice sacks. The big man asked about our health, observing that Beth had lost weight. We told him we were all in fine shape.

"Do you know why I have come?" he asked.

As the senior member of our group, I instructed Mike to reply that we did not know but that we hoped the reason was that the investigation had determined that we were, in fact, news correspondents, as we had claimed to be.

"Yes, that is it," he said. "The high command of the Cambodian nation has decided that you are to be released as soon as possible. Our inquiry took a long time because of the war situation. For the same reason, there is some difficulty over your belongings. We kept them together, but we don't know just now where they are or whether we will be able to return them to you. Will this create a serious problem for you?"

Mike told him that everything was replaceable and that they were of no importance under the circumstances.

"We will meet again in a few days and discuss how you can be returned safely to American control. In the meantime, it is not very good for you to stay here. I heard about the helicopters this afternoon. You will leave in a few minutes. It is a long hike. It will be difficult."

No danger or hardship seemed important now that we had been promised our freedom. We looked forward to a long march in the cool night air.

"Tomorrow," he went on, "I want you to write a statement in French telling what kind of treatment you have received since your arrest, your opinion of the Liberation Army, a comparison of the behavior of the Liberation Army with that of the American and Thieu-Ky forces, and what you think has been the result of the invasion of Cambodia. We can discuss some political questions, too, when we meet again. You will have an opportunity to speak with a representative of the Cambodian Liberation Army, who will answer your questions. In preparation for that meeting, you should write out questions in advance.

The North Vietnamese officer arose quietly, with the same warm smile. We shook hands and he wished us good luck. He and his aide stepped quietly down the ladder and moved off into the night.

Ba gave us a few final details about the march: "We must go twenty kilometers (about thirteen miles). There may be some bombing. We will have to move fast. Altogether the march should take about five hours."

At the foot of the ladder, Beth and Mike stepped into their sandals, and I hurriedly put on a pair of socks and my mud-caked shoes, tying them with the bits of laces that remained. Beth tied her sarong around her shoulders, to cover her light cotton shirt and to be ready to cover her head in an emergency. The guerrillas gave Mike a U.S. Army fatigue hat. Tu looked at my black beret and decided it did not obscure my Western face sufficiently. He traded me his broad-brimmed World War I-style dough-boy's hat for it and put the beret smartly over one eye. Ba gave Mike and me each one of the ten-pound salami-shaped cloth sacks of rice to sling across our shoulders. "Now if we see people they will think you are soldiers," he said. It reminded me of a device in the World War II novel *The Seventh Cross*, in which a fugitive making his way through a European city under the eyes of the Nazis carried a heavy piece of machinery to divert attention from himself and to make people think he had some legitimate reason for being there.

A new moon was beginning to set as we started out on the road along which we had often seen lines of soldiers passing during our two weeks in the base camp. Tu led the way, with Ba and Wang also up front. Beth, Mike, and I walked single file, with Ban Tun at one side, marching easily along with his heavy improvised knapsack of woven plastic. Hai brought up the rear.

The pale moonlight was bright enough at first to make it easy to keep to the path, which went in a straight line through open country and cut through an occasional forest. At one point, we met a line of perhaps one hundred guerrilla soldiers, each with his rifle and a pack. I thought I could make out pairs of heavy mortar shells or rockets in some of the packs. The moon went down, and we marched on in nearly total darkness, broken by the red spot of an occasional guerrilla cigarette. Beth's black pants were invisible, but the sight of her white ankles kept me from bumping into her. The bare packed dirt of the path shone with a dull whiteness against the grass and brush at each side of the trail, changing to a black patch wherever there was a puddle left over from the rain. No one spoke. There was just the soft shuffle of sandals, the slight squeak of my oxfords, the regular click of the strap of Mike's bag as it touched the ground with each step.

After a long stretch through the forest, we struck off at an angle on a road that led once more into the open between two canals. In the distance, we could see a row of flares marking U.S. firebases, their light reflected in a long checkerboard of rice paddies. I called Mike's attention to what looked like an elongated flare that stayed constantly in position instead of fading out like the others after five or ten minutes. It was a long row of bright lights just above the horizon. It seemed to be moving back and forth, much like the descriptions given of flying saucers. Mike thought it must be floodlights at the American base on top of Black Widow Mountain, the tall, conical mountain just across the border in South Vietnam near the city of Tay Ninh. At a rest stop, I lined up the light with my toe and saw the movement had been an optical illusion and he probably was right.

The stretch between the canals seemed endless. It must have gone on for three or four miles. As the canals dwindled out, we came to the most difficult part of all, a partly wrecked bridge. All the planking was gone, and it was so dark we could scarcely see the bare timbers or the water a few feet underneath. The others seemed to make it without difficulty, but the poor lighting made me dizzy and I had to inch along, pushing one foot ahead and bringing the other up to it until I at last reached the end of the long span, a good fifty yards.

Another mile or so, and we struck off along a winding path to the right. It skirted a house and led past a well to a larger house, where we could see figures silhouetted on a front porch against the light from a big doorway. It looked familiar, and I knew for sure where we were when we came to the broad steps of the heavy ladder we had climbed many times in the days we had spent at the Bug House. There was the grey-haired, erect man of the house, drinking his tea, with the teapot nearby in its coconut cozy. He smiled and returned our Buddhist greeting, palms together under the chin, and shook hands with us. Even his stern-faced wife, who had seemed grumpy and disapproving on our first visit and now had been routed out before dawn to make tea for a houseful of unexpected guests, gave us a hospitable smile.

We were tired, the guerrillas as well as the Americans, and we all slept until midday. Not even the beetles dropping from the ceiling could interfere with our sleep. When we finally awoke and went out of our little room into the main part of the house, Hai and Ban Tun were still motionless on their mats.

Ba, always mindful of his responsibility as military commander of our little task force, gave us terse instructions: "This area is relatively safe; the Americans know it is not suitable for our troops because there are no forests nearby where they could take refuge from an attack. We do not expect an attack, but if one should come anyhow don't try to run. Stay in this house. It is a strong one, and you are safest here. The danger of a direct hit is small."

Tu had picked up some news from the Cambodians: The

troops that had chased us out into the fields the morning after we had left the Bug House had missed us here by only five hours. When they passed through this hamlet, all the guerrillas had left. We could imagine the Cambodian family's innocent assurance that they had seen no Communist forces there for weeks.

He had some additional information about the attack on the first house where we had stayed, where we earlier had been told that the entire family had been killed. "Only the parents were killed," he said. "But the little girl had her arm shot off." The revised account of the incident was at the same time more poignant and more credible. By correcting the story, the guerrillas seemed to us to be passing along the best information they had. We took the incident as one more indication that they were straightforward in their dealings with us. Our growing confidence that we were not being made the victims of some trick enabled us to get to work that afternoon and agree on the statement that the big man had asked us to write without worrying too much about what use might be made of it. We knew they wanted it for propaganda purposes, but we were confident that we could write something that would be satisfactory to them without misrepresenting the truth as we had seen it. There would be places, we knew, where we could not speak of our own knowledge and where we would have to say that we were reporting what we had been told. I made a copy of the English draft after Beth had translated it into French:

Our treatment after our arrest on May 7, 1970, on Route 1 near Svai Rieng was generally very considerate of our safety and well-being. The only exception was an understandable incident on the first day, before our identity had been established. We were treated roughly (Beth translated this as "a little severely") for a time by the Cambodians, who we know have been led to hate all Americans by the invasion of Cambodia and the bombardment of the people by the Nixon Administration. These actions were halted by the authorities of the Liberation Army, who guaranteed our safety and promised to verify our statement that we were international journalists. We have suffered no bad effects from this incident.

Since that time, our treatment has been completely satisfactory. The men assigned to take care of us were very skillful and risked their lives to protect us against ground and air attack. They took good care of our health in sharing their food with us, obtaining medicines and toilet articles for us, and caring for our safety and welfare. Moreover, they showed sincere hospitality that made our stay with them agreeable and unforgettable.

The five weeks that we have passed with these soldiers have given us a very positive impression of the Liberation Army. We have observed particularly the relationship they have with the people. These soldiers were always polite and cordial to the civilians in the places they stayed. They paid for their food; they helped refugees flee danger zones; and they showed great respect for the families and homes where we stayed. For their part, the people showed friendship and generous cooperation to the soldiers.

We have also noted the high morale of the liberation soldiers, their clear understanding of their cause, and their profound dedication to its success. We have, more-

*over, observed their military competence, and we have
felt safe in their hands despite the dangerous circumstances.*

*These impressions of the liberation troops differ
sharply from our impression of the actions of the Saigon
troops on the day of our arrest. At Prasaut we saw that
these troops had carried away the city rice reserves as
well as furniture and other household effects. We noted
that these soldiers had broken into houses and stores
and stolen the contents. Most of the civilians had fled
the city or been killed. We were told that this is the
usual behavior of Saigon troops.*

*As for the Americans, we heard the sound of their
heavy bombing and the sound of machine guns and
rockets from their planes, as well as the sound of their
tanks and troops. We were told that many American
attacks, as well as those of Saigon troops, were directed
against civilian areas and that civilians were the principal
victims. We were told also of cases in which women
villagers were raped by American soldiers.*

*On the basis of our observations, we believe that the
invasion of Cambodia by American and Saigon troops
cannot be successful. It had done nothing except to
bring a bitter and prolonged war to a peaceful country
and has made peace in Indochina even more difficult to
achieve.*

If the English sounded in places like a bad translation
from another language, it was because in drafting we had
to keep in mind the limitations of Beth's French. She
sometimes stopped us with an objection that "I won't be

able to translate that," and we would back up and decide on an English phrase that she could handle.

With that assignment out of the way, we turned our attention to the questions we would ask at the final news conference we had been promised. We made them as specific as possible, asking for casualty figures on each side, the number of planes and helicopters shot down, how much territory and how much of the Cambodian population was considered under the control of the "Liberation Army." Turning to political questions, we noted that we had been told of their suspicions that the CIA had been involved in the overthrow of Sihanouk and asked for any factual information they could give us about this. We included an inquiry about the extent of cooperation among the peoples of Cambodia, Vietnam, and Laos in carrying on the different phases of their war of liberation; this was a way of trying to elicit something about the open secret that North Vietnam and the National Liberation Front had troops in Cambodia and clearly were directing the strategy and bearing the brunt of the fighting. Finally, we said that we would be asked immediately about other newsmen who were missing in Cambodia. We asked for any information that could be given about these correspondents or about American prisoners of war captured in Cambodia.

We turned the statement and questions over to Hai, and Mike and I directed our thoughts to something more urgent. Both of us had cramps and diarrhea, probably from some well water that Ban Tun had obtained from a house along our route the night before. After obtaining special permission twice to go outside to the makeshift latrine among the banana palms, I asked Ba if he had some medicine. Instead of the bitter white pills we had been given once before, Ba gave us a tiny bottle of Chinese medicine that smelled like oil of wintergreen. He had us rub some on our stomachs and then shook three drops into a glass of hot tea. It tasted like the inhalation of a menthol cigarette. I never had seen such a quick cure. The spasms stopped immediately, and there was no recurrence.

The next day, June 11, Hai and Ba spent several hours talking with us about the nature of their revolution and the importance of journalists in telling the story of that revolution to the world. The time of our release was fast approaching, and they wanted to influence what we wrote about our experience, whether out of personal dedication to their cause or out of bureaucratic awareness that they would get the blame or credit for the accounts we gave. Yet their rambling discussions were no hard-sell summation; rather, they were relaxed talks among friends, as we sat on the polished slatted floor and drank one little cup of tea after another and occasionally munched Ban Tun's green guavas.

"All we want is for you to write the reality of our situation here," Hai told us. "Although people say many things about us, our goals are very simple. What we want are better societies, factories owned by the people, construction of more schools, and the provision of medicines for the people."

There was a pause, and Ba reminded us of some of the things we had gone through: "You have shared many experiences with us. We have eaten rice and salt, and we have eaten rice with other things that were strange

to you. We have drunk tea, hot water, cold water, and
water that made us sick. We have hidden in the forest from
planes and helicopters, and we have marched twenty kilometers in a single night."

Hai, wearing his black pajama pants and his undershirt
turned up to ventilate his back and stomach, took over the
conversation and described the peoples of the world as
being like a single family. "We are all brothers, although
we live far apart and under different influences," he said.
The revolutionist is a special type—he must have a great
spirit of sacrifice. Writers and journalists have perhaps the
most important role of making people aware of their own
situations. They also can make the meaning of revolution
clear to those who are so harried by their day-to-day social
and economic pressures that they have neither the time
nor the inclination to think much about abstract things
like the making of revolution."

We could hear bombs exploding in the distance and the
occasional faint chatter of machine guns. But the war
seemed far away as we listened to his soft Vietnamese
voice and felt the light midday breeze that swayed the
banana palms outside and swept through the big open
house.

"Life does not move along an even path," the veteran
revolutionary went on. "There are times of pleasure and
times of pain, times of danger and times of comfort and
security. The most important thing, through it all, is
friendship and helpfulness along the way. When we help
someone else, the favor is always returned, not necessarily
to ourselves but maybe much later to our son." He paused
again. "There are imperialism and oppression in the world,

but there also is progress in the world. A great world revolution is coming that will destroy imperialism and bring a better life for everyone."

When we were left alone, Mike proposed that we present each of the guerrillas with some small gift and that I, as the senior member of our little group, make the presentation. I raised the question of whether we should tip off Hai in advance so as not to embarrass them by a surprise, but Mike said, "Don't worry, they'll be up to the situation."

Later that afternoon, when dinner was over and we were drinking tea, I startled the guerrillas by telling them through Mike that I had something to say to them and wished they would wait until I got something from my room. When I returned with the items we had selected packed into a coconut shell and covered with my old beret, I made my speech, with Mike translating a sentence or two at a time.

"It is exactly five weeks that we have been with you," I began. "We want to express our appreciation for the way you have looked after our health and safety and, still more important, for your offer of friendship. This is to say nothing of several times when you actually have saved our lives. Now, these things are impossible to repay, and we would not try to repay them. But we do have some small and insignificant mementos that we would like to leave with you now that the time of our stay with you is coming to an end."

The guerrillas watched intently as I spoke and listened carefully to Mike's translation. We sat cross-legged in a circle, Mike, Beth and I at one side.

Starting with Chi Tinh, the nurse who had been with us

for the first two weeks, I recalled that she had talked to us about the revolution and had given us medicine when we needed it. "For her, Beth would like to leave her scarf, and we hope you can see that she gets it, together with this list of our names and addresses." I handed Hai the small brown silk scarf that they had seen Beth wear tied into her ponytail almost every day. Hai took it without a word and laid it on the floor in front of him.

Ban Tun came next in reverse order of rank, and I tried to make a little joke about the friendly Cambodian. "We will always remember him as a good soldier and a good friend," I said, "but we also will remember him as the one who brought us many fruits and vegetables—some of them very sweet and some very bitter." The guerrillas laughed as they recalled Ban Tun's wild oranges, so sticky and bitter that Ba had torn part of the paper tea sack into bits, one for each of us to use to try to wipe the juice off our teeth. "So we would like him to have the little pocket knife to help him peel the fruits and vegetables he will gather from here on. But there is a small problem. We have a superstition in America that the gift of a knife can ruin a friendship. So I will give Ban Tun also an American penny that I found in my bag, and we consider that the knife is a purchase rather than a gift."

Wang, the Chinese student from Phnom Penh, had always admired my chromium-plated nail clippers from a PX in Saigon. I reminded them that he was something of a dude and said the nail clippers were to help him keep himself attractive for the girls. For Tu, I recalled his leading us along paths through fields and forests at night, always wearing his broad-brimmed hat, his blue shirt, and his green pants, walking as quietly as a mouse or an owl. "Although the broad-brimmed hat is an essential part of the picture, we hope he will wear this beret sometimes and remember our times together."

Ba, in his spotless khaki uniform, was waiting impassively for his turn. "For Ba," I said, "the skillful soldier who saved our lives two days ago as well as on the day we arrived, we want to leave the key to Mike's house in Saigon as a symbol of the fact that all of you are welcome at our homes as long as we live." Mike passed him the brass key. Ba handed it to Hai, who placed it in a row in front of him with the other gifts, each on the piece of paper that told the recipient and listed our names.

"And now we come to Hai," I went on, "a perfect leader for this little group that has taken such good care of us. We will remember him as an explainer of the revolution, as a giver of the day's news, as an excellent cook, but especially as a chess player. We leave you our chess men so that you can continue to play after we leave." I passed him the chess men, tied up in one of my handkerchiefs.

"Now these are crudely made, and they will not last very long, since they are carved of green wood," I continued. "We hope that, in comparison with their short life, the remaining life of this war will be even shorter and that by the time they have fallen to pieces your struggle for freedom and independence will have reached its successful conclusion."

Mike was right about the guerrillas' *savoir faire*. Hai was ready with a speech in reply. He spoke quietly and earnestly, pausing from time to time for Mike to translate. He said: "We understand that these things do not have much value. They are very simple little mementos. But in another way they are very important. For example, the key that you have given us means that any time I want I can go right into your house. It means that your house is my house. It symbolizes that we all are very close friends."

He went on: "Do not think that we don't understand your meaning in giving us these things. We understand clearly. If you had tried to give us money, it would have meant very little. But these things mean a great deal to us. You should not be sad because we give them back to you. In giving them back to you, we give them as our belongings. We hope that when you use each one of these things you will think of them as things that we have given to you and will remember each of us when you use them." He then picked up each of the gifts, commented on it, set it back in place and turned to Ba.

Ba said: "Let me first say that we thank you very much for this thoughtfulness. During these weeks that we have been together, it has been our greatest concern that you remain healthy and happy. When you have been sick or listless, we also have been sad because we felt that we were not taking good enough care of you. We consider you not as prisoners of war but as travelers who have lost their way. If we had had advance notice of your coming and if your identity had been clear, or if there were peace, we could have done much more to take care of you. But now, as you are preparing to go back to your country or back to your work, in our eyes you have crossed over and we now consider you as our friends."

We were puzzled and a little hurt over Hai's refusal of the gifts. We understood that face was involved, that modesty and humility are among the highest virtues in East Asia and that to return a gift that you would like to keep is more honorable that to accept it. We suspected that the revolutionary concept of eschewing physical possessions and denying any interest in material things also was involved.

Ba saw our disappointment and seemed to try to find a formula that would permit the guerrillas to accept them: "Normally it is our custom to give a memento in return when something is given to us. But we feel in this case, because you must go back to the other side and must go through a period of danger and difficulty, it is better that we not give you anything extra to carry. We will discuss this matter with our superiors, and perhaps we can arrange for you to get mementos from us later on."

Living with them for five weeks, we had seen all their spartan belongings and knew that they had nothing at all to spare as farewell gifts. There was some talk between the two men, and Hai again attempted an explanation. He told Mike: "You have married a Vietnamese girl, and you know the custom of taking two or three thousand piasters to her family and how her family returns exactly the same amount in gifts to your family so that everybody gets something and nobody loses anything. This is the Vietnamese custom, the Asian custom, and so we must give these gifts back to you. All but the chessmen—we watched you carve while you were with us, and we will be happy to keep them here after you go. One at a time, he put the scarf, the knife and penny, the nail clippers and the key into the beret. He took the chess men from the handker-

chief and kept them. Then he folded the handkerchief
neatly, added it to the things in the beret, and passed them
across to me. He said:

*We have been able to meet in circumstances that
normally would have prevented us from becoming
acquainted with one another. We have grown to know
one another. Soon there will be a great distance between
us, but we will not forget you. We all belong to society,
and the intellectuals have an important role to play even
when our revolution has succeeded. We will be thinking
of you and the revolutionary movement abroad, outside
of our own countries in Indochina. Human society is
like one of our little oil lamps, with its wick and top and
bottle and oil and other parts. Every part has its func-
tion, and each part is essential to enable the lamp to
produce light. The intellectuals are very important in
human society. As I told you before, you can explain
our revolution to the poor and oppressed peoples of the
world.*

*We will remember you in two ways. First, by strug-
gling hard to bring independence and freedom to our
people, to end aggression and slavery in our country.
Secondly, we shall listen carefully to the radio for news
of the articles you will write. We have two hopes for
you: first, that we can meet again when peace has come
and, second, that you will become leaders of the revolution in your own countries—if not big leaders, then
small leaders. Many of the American troops who have
been fighting in Vietnam will return home prepared to*

*work for revolutionary changes in the United States,
just as many Algerians who were forced to fight on the
side of the French in Indochina returned and made a
revolution in Algeria.*

*We hope that you will return to America and Canada
and will tell the political leaders, the Senators, and the
people about your experiences here and what we are
really like. If it were not for what Nixon is doing and if
it were not for the American aggression and all the
difficulties caused by this war, we would have peace and
your stay could have been much more pleasant.*

The ceremony was over, and the others drifted off to
other parts of the house, all but Tu, who sat down again
with us and asked if we would like to see a picture of his
wife. He took from his pocket a plastic picture case and
opened it to the photograph of a pretty Vietnamese girl.
The print was stained and faded. "She gave it to me five
years ago," he said. "It lasted well, but the water got to it
the night the truck got stuck. Some of the pictures got wet
and I had to lay them out to dry." Another picture
showed his wife and a little girl—"with a dark skin like
mine."

"I feel very sad about my wife and little girl. My wife
died two months ago at Prasaut. I cannot take care of my
daughter and I don't see her for long periods and cannot
know how she is getting along. But I feel that I cannot
fulfill my responsibilities as a father until the country has
been liberated, until American aggression has ended and
the people have been freed from slavery. I may be an old

man before I can fulfill my family responsibilities, but that is the way I feel.

"This is a fundamental fact of the revolution. The wives are usually dead or separated from their husbands. Families are secondary. Family obligations are very strong in Vietnam, but they must be postponed indefinitely. The only reward is the success of the revolution, and this may not come to oneself but only to the movement.

"The women of Vietnam like the liberation soldiers very much. They want to marry them and start families with them. But the liberation soldiers are all afraid that they will die." He smiled as he always did when he spoke seriously. "My wife was always worried about me. She was always afraid I would be killed. But as it turned out she died and I lived. It is quite possible that the struggle will cost our lives. But there will always be others to replace us. Our movement will win in the end."

Ban Tun came up as Tu spoke. The Cambodian had understood only snatches of what had been said in Vietnamese, but he was intensely interested in Tu's photographs. He took the case and looked carefully at the picture of Tu's wife. Tu told him in Cambodian, with his sad smile, "She's dead." Ban Tun pondered that for a moment and then said, "My wife is dead, too." He took the folder of pictures over to the side door that looked out on the coconut palms in the late afternoon sunshine, turned on the transistor radio, and lay down looking at the picture of Tu's wife for a half-hour, lost in thought.

10
farewell

"Where would you prefer to be released?" Hai asked. "I don't know yet what the possibilities are, but I would like to know your preference."

Between games of chess with Tu with the new set of men we had given him, Hai was busy preparing for the dangerous operation of transferring us back to American control.

We consulted a moment and told him our first choice would be Hanoi. We had talked this over many times and had decided that a visit to the North Vietnamese capital would be the best climax to the experience. It also would provide a good look at the length of the Ho Chi Minh trail. We knew of no Westerner who had given a first-hand report about the infiltration route that started as a system of trails and under continual American bombing had been improved until it now could carry heavy truck traffic much of the way through Laos into South Vietnam. Our second choice was Vientiane; our third, Saigon, and our last, Phnom Penh. Mike had been intrigued by the thought of having the guerrillas slip us into the heart of Saigon, a feat that we thought they probably could accomplish with the help of underground agents and forged passes.

"It would be a long and difficult trip to go to Hanoi," Hai said. "There is much fighting between here and there. We will decide what is the best place when the time comes." In the meantime, he said, there were some preliminaries. A photographer was coming and would want to take some pictures of us together, possibly a guerrilla-American chess game. Hai asked us to have the other gifts ready so we could lay them out on the floor for another picture. In the afternoon, he said, we all would have another feast with dog as the main course.

The photographer arrived early the next morning—Saturday, June 13—one of a half-dozen men who had come from some headquarters post in the region to make arrangements for our release. The photographer was the same talkative fellow who had accompanied Hai when he joined our party a week after our capture. Another in the group was the unpleasant little French-speaking man with the buck teeth, who shielded his mouth with one hand when he spoke and who had complained that our cameras looked more like spy cameras than press cameras. This time, however, he was friendly, having been given the word that we had passed muster and were going to be released.

The cameraman wanted to get started right away. I headed for our room to get the gifts to use as props, but

Hai told us the plans had been changed. The pictures would not show the gifts or a game of chess; in fact, they would show no Vietnamese at all. He was suddenly very businesslike, having shed the easy informality that he had developed during the weeks we had spent together. The change may have been partly that he had been overruled on the photographic plans. Beyond that, the new arrivals might not understand it if they saw him fraternizing with prisoners. But still more important, I think, was the fact that the eight of us, the three correspondents and the five guerrillas, had come to think of ourselves as a group of friends. The others were outsiders, who interfered with the relaxed routine we had come to enjoy.

Ban Tun, the Cambodian soldier, was the only one of the five who was to be photographed with us. The photographer had us put on "Ho Chi Minh sandals," made of automobile tires, and line up in front of the house. Then he outfitted Ban Tun with a pistol and belt, the first time the Cambodian had been permitted to wear this symbol of officer's rank, and placed him in front of us, holding a rifle, as if he were guarding us. The idea, of course, was that the Cambodians were running the guerrilla operations in Cambodia. This play-acting seemed at first to be an imposition on Ban Tun, who always had done the menial jobs like hauling wood and water. But he continued to wear the pistol the rest of the day and thereafter. He drew more responsible assignments and seemed to have been promoted to officer.

Back inside the house, the photographer turned on a stream of conversation, some of it indiscreet and some of it so silly that he later corrected himself. One indiscretion was an implied admission that Communist-led Vietnamese troops had entered Cambodia and were doing most of the fighting. What he said was, "We do not look upon our coming here to help the Cambodians as aggression or expanding our own country. We look upon it as helping a poor and oppressed people to resist aggression."

He knew that I was from Washington and wanted to know if I was acquainted with Senator Fulbright. I said I was. "You must tell him for me," he said, "that what he needs is not many strategies but just one strategy. He should go and live and work with the poor and oppressed. Where there is poverty and oppression, there is war. Where poverty and oppression are eliminated, there is peace." A little later, possibly after one of the others had spoken to him about it, he returned to the subject and said, "Before you give that message to Senator Fulbright, I would like to check it with my superiors, because I am just an ordinary soldier."

This nonstop talker gave us a quick story of his career. He said he was thirty years old and had been with the revolution for six years, as an underground agent in Saigon before coming to Cambodia to join in the fighting. He said he took part in the first attack by the National Liberation Front against the Americans, a strike against the U.S. Twenty-fifth Division at Cu Chi on January 7, 1965.

"I have two sisters who are secret agents in Saigon," he said. "One throws plastic bombs from a motorbike. I know other girls who have an assignment to shoot Americans while riding on the back of motorbikes. I know one girl who can shoot a pistol with either hand from the back of a motorbike."

An amateur philosopher, he gave us his slant on the underlying nature of the revolutionary movement. "To make the revolution effectively," he said, "we must have two main qualities, ideals and hatred. We hate the imperialists and the aggressors in America but not the poor and oppressed there; if we saw them we would embrace them as brothers. And in the American Army, we know that some of the soldiers do not want to fight against us but have been drafted into service and ordered to do so. Unfortunately, in a war situation we cannot distinguish them from the others."

He instructed the three of us how best to conduct ourselves once we got back to our homes. To me, he said: "Your work as a commentator is very important and can affect the thinking of people throughout the world." To Mike and Beth, he said: "I advise you to study socialism and become leaders of the progressive movement in America. And you should visit the socialist countries; to visit only the capitalist countries does not teach you about the whole world." He advocated the new "engaged" journalism and told us, "When you get back, you must not only write politics but also choose sides. And when you choose sides, you must always support the revolution. In fact, you two (indicating Mike and me) should start a new newspaper dedicated to revolution." He advised Beth to become a revolutionary leader of the American women.

The pair from the higher headquarters, the photographer and the French-speaking man, brought in a plastic sack of papers, which we saw were the various statements and articles we had written, and began looking through them to find some suitable things for us to read into a tape recorder. They were all there, including Mike's articles that we had been told had already been sent off somewhere for transmission to his syndicate's representative in Washington—all, that is, except for the letters we had written to our families. Maybe this meant they actually had been sent and Helen and the girls already knew I was safe.

Hai told us they wanted to record our voices as a "memento." We didn't contradict him, although we knew they must be preparing for a propaganda broadcast. Mike picked out his first dispatch, about our first few days with the guerrillas and what we had seen of their good relationship with the Cambodian people. I chose the statement that Mike, Beth, and I had drafted. As we read them into a Japanese tape recorder, the microphone must also have picked up a yelping and squealing under the house as someone went about killing the dog for dinner.

We had no particular qualms about the prospect of having our statements broadcast. We had written them carefully, sticking to the truth as we saw it, although at the same time trying to avoid offending the guerrillas. My only hesitancy was over the reference to reports that American troops had raped Cambodian women, but we knew that such things were happening in the course of the war and, besides, it was strictly speaking true, as we said, that we had been *told* that those incidents had taken place.

I did regret Hai's disingenuousness in saying that the taping was for a memento. But after the recording session was over he corrected himself. "We may broadcast your statements," he said, "but only after we know that you are safe." The guerrillas thus maintained their apparently perfect record of being candid with us. Several times we had suspected possible entrapment or deception, but our suspicions always had turned out to be unfounded. We had feared that we would be forced to rewrite our dossiers many times as a way of tricking us into contradicting ourselves. When I was being run blindfolded the first afternoon, and again when Twitch and I were hiding in the brush during the first attack, I thought for sure I was going to be shot in the back of the head. When we were invited to write articles, I was afraid we were being trapped into a permanent role as captive propagandists. None of these suspicions and fears proved out.

The realization that these guerrillas were trustworthy reminded me of a conversation I had in 1969 with a member of the Lower House of the South Vietnamese Congress, a man named Huong Ho. One night, as we sat together in his modest home back of a store in downtown Saigon, he told me how he had fought against the French with the Viet Minh but after 1954 had decided to settle in the South because he did not want to live under Communist rule. But with some regret and disillusionment he told me how he missed the members of the National Liberation Front, the successors to the Viet Minh. They were not venal or corrupt the way so many officials were in the South. He said they put the Vietnamese nationalist independence movement ahead of their own interests. I remembered that he described them as "pure."

We had come to know the guerrillas pretty well by this time. As I told Mike, it might sound corny, but they seemed to have all the standard virtues that are valued in Western society. I recalled the titles of the Boy Scout Laws that I had memorized as a boy: A Scout is Trustworthy,

Loyal, Helpful, Friendly, Courteous, Kind, Obedient, Cheerful, Thrifty, Brave, Clean, and Reverent. They all fitted the guerrillas perfectly except possibly for the last, and, although they were atheists, their devotion to their cause could be considered a form of reverence.

Where their brand of morality and ethics affected us most directly was that they always respected our rights. We were never coerced or even asked to write or say anything we considered untrue, nor were we asked to sign anything formulated by anyone else.

After the recording session, the French-speaking man indicated that he wanted to talk privately with us in our room. With some apparent embarrassment, he brought up the matter of our cameras and other belongings. They had been cached in the house where we had stayed the first few nights, and the guerrillas had left them there when we fled just ahead of a South Vietnamese attack. They had thought they might be able to return later for them, but the South Vietnamese troops had found them and taken them, he said. Not knowing whether to believe the story or not, we told him anyhow that the things were of no great importance and could best be forgotten.

"We feel bad about taking anything at all from you— even this cookie," he said. We had given him a cookie left over from a special treat at breakfast, and he had accepted it only reluctantly and had carefully left it uneaten on the floor beside him. "I feel bad about your belongings, because you are good people. If you had been bad people I would gladly have killed you and kept your belongings."

As that bit of meanness was sinking in, he unexpectedly took a stack of currency from his pocket and counted out five new 1000-piaster South Vietnamese banknotes for each of us plus a tattered grey 100-riel Cambodian note for each. "I have been instructed to give you this money so that you will not be stranded on your way to Saigon. You will be released on Route 1, and you may need money for food or for a taxicab." We objected to taking any money—the whole amount came to roughly $50—but he insisted.

Our next visitor was Ban Tun, who brought Wang along as an interpreter. The Cambodian soldier, whom we had come to know mostly through jokes and games, explained that the language difficulty had kept us from becoming well acquainted. "Before you go, I want to ask you some questions about yourselves and your country," he said. "What families do you have? When you return to America, will it be peaceful and will you be safe there? And will you write about your experiences when you return home?"

After absorbing Mike's answers, Ban Tun told us something of his own story: "Before the March 18 coup, Cambodia was peaceful and prosperous. I was an officer in Lon Nol's personal guard at the Prime Ministry. I quit the day before the coup to become a plain soldier in Prince Sihanouk's revolutionary army. My company was the closest to the prime minister, and we all deserted. I had to leave my wife and two daughters. She was expecting our third child about now. I have heard that my children are still in Phnom Penh, but I have heard no word of my wife. Maybe they are all killed by this time. I intend to fight with the liberation army until Lon Nol is defeated and Prince Sihanouk and the former policy of neutrality have been restored."

Ban Tun said he was not a Communist and knew very

little about the Khmer Rouge, the Cambodian Communist faction that had existed for many years and now was cooperating with the North Vietnamese and the National Liberation Front. Cambodians who had joined the Cambodian Front included a few Communists, but, as he put it, they were mostly "capitalists."

He went on to say that, when the United States and the Saigon government came to the support of Lon Nol's new regime, it was obvious that the Cambodian Front could not succeed by itself but must have help from "the people of Laos, the North Vietnamese nation, and the National Liberation Front of South Vietnam." He said, "We four peoples, in solidarity, must oppose Lon Nol, the Americans, the Saigon regime, and Thailand."

Before continuing, Ban Tun wanted an answer to a specific question: "Did the American people know about the March eighteenth coup against Prince Sihanouk before it happened?" He and all the other guerrillas with whom we talked were convinced that the CIA had engineered the coup, and the photographer and the French-speaking guerrilla had brought new circumstantial detail as further proof of U.S. government complicity. They had said that two officials of the American embassy were with Lon Nol at the exact moment of the coup and that Adam Malik, the foreign minister of Indonesia, had gone to Cambodia just before the coup and helped arrange it as an agent of the CIA. Whatever the facts of the matter—and the story about Malik did not ring true at all—I was able to assure him that the American people had no idea the coup was going to take place.

"If it is true that the American people did not knowingly support the overthrow of Prince Sihanouk and are opposing what their government is doing here now, the effort cannot succeed," he said. "But the withdrawal of U.S. troops from Cambodia by itself will not be enough to bring peace. The Thieu-Ky troops also must be withdrawn. The affairs of Cambodia must be determined by the Cambodians, and the affairs of Indochina must be determined by the people of Indochina, without outside interference. Only when Prince Sihanouk is restored to power and when peace and neutrality are restored to Cambodia will I return to my family. We are all in the same situation, since we are all far away from our families. I am glad to have met you American journalists, who will write against the American aggression in Cambodia. I am sorry that I don't speak Vietnamese or French or English and that there has been a mask between us. But I am glad to have been with you while you have been here."

We were touched by the carefully thought out speech from this soldier who we had thought was probably not handy with words. Beth, who had taken a special liking to him, made a warm response. Through Mike, she told him, "There is a language of friendship and helpfulness and trust that doesn't require words. We've said a great deal to each other in this other language."

Our five guerrillas seemed to draw closer to us as the time of our departure approached. This was partly a reaction to the visitors from headquarters, who continued to talk with us in slogans. Hai found time for a chat before dinner, and he made a point that might have been taken as a sensible piece of advice by a Roger Hilsman or a Robert Komer or other Americans who had ever thought the war worth winning but were critical of American strategy. "We're different from the Americans," Hai said. "We shoot only when we have a target. The Americans often shoot at empty places or at places where there are civilians but no Liberation soldiers. This not only wastes money, but it actually promotes American failure, since it destroys lives and property and turns the people against the United States."

The dog banquet that had been in preparation for several hours turned out to be a formal affair. Twenty plates were laid out in two rows on the floor, some borrowed from the neighbors as well as the enamelware dishes we had been using every day, decorated with flowers and with the label "Peoples' Republic of China" on the back. In the center were three big pots of steaming rice and three sets of side dishes—braised dog, dog soup with melon, bits of fried dog, ground peanuts mixed with a fish paste, a bean paste, and boiled greens, as well as bowls of salt and pepper. As we sat cross-legged and reached for big helpings of rice and then spooned up meat and seasonings from the side dishes, I counted three Americans, twelve Vietnamese, and five Cambodians at the table. Beth was the only woman there; several Cambodian women sat back from the table and watched in silence. Hardly a word was spoken. Only the old Cambodian man of the house said more than a word or two. He made a very brief speech as host, saying, "You will be leaving soon. We will miss you when you go." We replied that we had enjoyed coming to know them and would think of them often. Even the rice wine, poured into a single glass and passed from hand to hand, did not break the ice.

The easy informality returned the next morning, when we had leftover dog for breakfast with our five guerrillas. For a joke, one of them put the dog's head on my plate when I turned away for a moment. "We eat in solidarity," Ba said with a smile. I laughed it off and put the head on Ba's plate, saying to Mike, "Tell him that solidarity goes just so far and no farther."

Mike had an inspiration that it would be fun to write a guerrilla cookbook and put in all the strange things we had been eating lately. He and Hai went over by the big open door and talked quietly for an hour about the project while Mike made notes. Whenever Mike's Vietnamese was not up to the task and there was some doubt, Hai took the pen and paper and wrote in Chinese, so that Mike's wife could make a correct translation when he got back to Saigon.

As we waited for our press conference, Tu, Ba, and Wang each came to us with a small piece of paper bearing his correct name and the best he could do for a permanent address, either in Phnom Penh or Saigon, and said to keep it secret for the present but to try to get in touch again after the war was over. It was the only time we were requested to withhold information after our release.

The press conference was obviously considered very important. From time to time all day, Mike had overheard Hai and others discussing written questions we had submitted and formulating the answers. After lunch, he asked us to dress in light-colored clothing, possibly to show up better in photographs. For me, that meant my white pants and polo shirt. We combed our hair and waited. At about noon we were led through backyards to a neighboring house that we had not seen before. It was one of the few structures we had seen with cement front steps instead of the usual ladder, and inside we found a half-dozen chairs, a rarity in the peasant homes where we had been staying. Ba, Tu, and Ban Tun, armed with rifles and pistols, ushered us into the main room, where a table had been covered with a pink plastic tablecloth and decorated with two plastic flowers in tin cans covered with shiny blue paper. Behind the table and behind three chairs that had been placed facing it for us, there were two revolutionary flags, the first we had seen. They were the Cambodian national flag—a red field bearing a white drawing of the chief temple at Angkor Wat, with a broad blue stripe at the top and bottom—with the letters F.U.N.K., for *Front Uni National du Kampuchea* (the United National Front of Cambodia) superimposed. A young Cambodian man, smoking a banana-leaf marijuana cigar, lounged in the doorway. The woman of the house, tall and handsome, holding one child and pregnant with another, watched from the door of a bedroom and chewed betel nut, occasionally spitting red saliva down through the slats to the ground. Ducks quacked and a cow chewed its cud under the house. From time to time there was a chatter of distant machine guns and the boom of artillery that shook the petals of the plastic flowers. An observation plane droned overhead and went on.

The photographer talked continuously, giving us a stream of dubious information about the incidents of the war, usually featuring his heroic part in them. Tu set out a pot of tea and five big beer glasses.

At last there was a stir and we saw eight armed men

walking single file along a path toward the house. Among them was Ironface, the counterintelligence agent who had interrogated us so sternly; I hardly recognized him at first, because he smiled at us. A Cambodian and a Vietnamese took seats behind the table. The Cambodian wore a blue bandana around his neck, opened a school composition book before him and introduced himself as the commander of the 203rd military region. He spoke in Cambodian, and the Vietnamese, who wore a red bandana at this throat, translated into French. We interrupted to ask the Cambodian's name and rank and the location of the 203rd military region. He replied that he could not give us that information for reasons of military security. A Vietnamese placed a microphone in front of him and turned on a tape recorder, and the press conference began.

It started as more of a speech than a press conference. The Cambodian would read several sentences from the notebook and then wait impatiently for the translation as we wrote furiously to try to keep up and the photographer snapped pictures. The Cambodian began, "The patriotic spirit and the spirit of liberty of the Khmer people is nothing other than the spirit of the people of the world," and continued like that for about twenty minutes. I was afraid we were in for nothing but polemics. Later, however, he began to include some statements of fact that showed an effort to answer most of our questions. We had no way of knowing at the time the truth of most of what he said but considered it worth reporting in a war in which credibility is often lacking on all sides.

He claimed that the revolutionary front forces controlled three entire provinces in eastern Cambodia—Kratie,

Stung Treng, and Mondul Kiri—with a total population of
two million, as well as forty district capitals outside the
three provinces. Turning to an Esso road map of Cambodia
pinned to the wall behind him, he pointed out the areas
where he said the F.U.N.K. forces held control. Another
interesting bit was that he described the Front as being
"under the direction of the Communist Party in Cambodia." This was a reference to the Khmer Rouge.

The Cambodian commander's statement included a long
list of charges of CIA intervention. He said that CIA agents
had infiltrated the Cambodian government, as well as the
Phnom Penh diplomatic missions of France, Australia,
Japan, Saigon, and Formosa, and engineered Sihanouk's
overthrow. He claimed that the Front forces had "put out
of action" 40,000 troops since March 18, including 3,000
Americans and 20,000 troops of the "Saigon puppet regime." He listed American, South Vietnamese, and Thai
units that he said were taking part in the invasion.

He denounced past American efforts to overthrow
Sihanouk, tracing these plots back to 1955. He blamed
President Nixon personally for the invasion of Cambodian
territory, distinguishing the government from the people
of the United States. "The imperialistic regime of the
American government is utterly savage," he said. "It does
not allow the people of Indochina to live in peace. It is
more fascist that the Hitler regime, trying to transform
Indochina into a new colony under its domination."

The commander made no response to two of our most
important questions, what assistance the peoples of Indochina might give each other in the war and what he could
tell us about other news correspondents missing in Cam-

bodia. Nor was there any answer to our question about word of any American military men who might have been captured in Cambodia.

The statement took two hours to read, slowed as it was by translation. The Cambodian began to cut the translation short toward the end, and when he finished he said there was no time for questions. He shook hands and strode off down the path, followed by Ironface and the rest of his group, together with the photographer and the French-speaking guerrilla. Suddenly we were left alone with our old friends, Tu, Ba, and Ba Tun. At ease after the formalities with the higher echelon, Tu and Ba sat down behind the table in mock seriousness and pretended to start another press conference. "Where's the photographer?" Ba asked, pretending to pose for a picture. We all laughed, and Ba slapped Mike on the knee and said something that Mike said could be translated, "Well, that's that," in the manner of subordinates all over the world when the brass has left.

Back at the other house, we learned that we would take off in mid-afternoon, not waiting for nightfall. Ba made us each a small truce flag, using my two handkerchiefs and another square of white cloth and tying them neatly to small bamboo sticks. He rolled them carefully and told us to keep them ready to display as we made our way across to the other side. Our instructions in case of attack were now to be different. "Don't run with us. Just show yourselves and hold up your flags," he said. "We will run the other way."

"*Chuan bi di,*" Ba said, for what we thought would be the last time. The eight of us, three Americans and five guerrillas, picked up our bags and packs, said goodby to the Cambodian farmer and his family, and marched off through the backyards to a road where a small taxi-bus was waiting. It seemed strange to be traveling in the daytime.

We drove for an hour, until we reached a large village. Crowds of people were streaming in from the surrounding countryside. They were gathering on the parade ground in front of an elementary school. Our taxi-bus pulled to a stop on the grounds, and we realized that this was a mass meeting. We were led to a table at one side of a speaker's platform. Two lines of twenty Cambodian guerrilla soldiers, armed with a motley collection of Communist-made and captured American carbines, rifles, and machine guns, held back the crowd to form an open area. I took off my beret, and there was a ripple of laughter at the unaccustomed sight of a bald head. Most of the people there had never seen a Westerner, much less a bald-headed one. Facing the speaker's stand were red and blue banners held on poles, with gold letters that said things like, "Long live the Khmer people," and, "Long live the solidarity of the Indochina people." One that appeared to be brand new said, "We thank the American people who support our struggle for independence." I estimated the crowd at two thousand.

An officer stepped to the microphone and made a short speech, the main point of which was an expression of thanks "to the American people who support our struggle." He went on: "Unfortunately, the American people have at their head Richard Nixon, who is an aggressor."

Storm clouds had been gathering, and a driving monsoon rainstorm broke up the meeting just as Beth was making a polite response. The crowd applauded and broke and ran for cover in the deepening dusk, and we were guided onto the school porch to escape the downpour. One of the guerrillas told us to step through a narrow doorway into the school, I thought for further protection against the storm. But in the dark classroom, we found ourselves at a school table facing our old acquaintance, the tall North Vietnamese officer whom we always seemed to see at crucial moments in this adventure, his face visible by the dim light of his flashlight. With him was the Cambodian commander from the press conference. The North Vietnamese took charge. After shaking hands warmly, he repeated the final instructions about using our truce flags and gave us each a safe-conduct pass. It was a typed, signed statement on onion-skin paper. The writing was Cambodian, but we could make out our three names near the top. "Show these to any other Front forces that you may encounter," he said, "but by no means show them to any Cambodian, Vietnamese, or American troops on your way to Saigon."

"Unfortunately," he went on, "the rain will make the roads impassable from here to Route 1. You will have to return to the house where you have been staying and start out again tomorrow." With a twinkle, he added, "When you come next time to the Liberated Zone, please be sure to wait for an invitation and we'll be able to take better care of you." He wished us good luck, and he and the Cambodian officer left by another door.

Outside on the porch, it was still raining hard. Hai stepped up and said that he would be leaving us. Mike and I shook hands with him and then embraced him. Beth extended her hand and gave him every opportunity to kiss it, but he backed away in embarrassment, said goodby, and hiked off to rejoin the revolution. Ban Tun, too, was leaving—for another assignment, but first for a few days' leave in which he hoped to find his family in Phnom Penh—and there was a similar farewell to him except that he let Beth kiss him goodby. Tu seemed most affected of all at the parting. He gave us each a hug and said he was sure we would see each other again when the war was over.

Now it was just three Americans and two guerrillas. As we drove back through the rain, we stopped briefly in the village for Wang to buy two plastic sacks of those Cambodian crullers for a bedtime snack. We ate them with tea and some of Ba's emergency rations of sticky rice molded into balls and dipped into a mixture of salt, sugar, and pepper. As we ate, Ba gave us some new information about the series of unexpected moves we had made in the first two weeks. We had left the first house, where the shy little girl had peeked in at us, just two hours before the start of the attack. He said the Thieu-Ky forces had bombarded the hamlet with 100 rounds of 105-millimeter shells and then advanced on the ground in jeeps and tanks. At the Barn, where we had fled in mid-afternoon, an attack had come two days later. And at the old man's hut, which we had left in the middle of the night, the attack had come next morning at dawn.

"We always know when there is going to be an attack," Ba said. "We can tell by watching the planes and by getting reports of troop movements on the ground." His explanation seemed more persuasive than the more spectacular supposition sometimes heard that spies at military headquarters overhear the secret plans and pass the word to the guerrillas in the field.

We set out again the next afternoon, this time in an open Jeep instead of the taxi-bus. Ba sat in the front seat, natty as always in his creased khakis and his khaki-colored pith helmet, and wearing his square blue sunglasses with steel rims. Crowded in with him were a Cambodian driver and a Cambodian rifleman. In the back, besides Beth, Mike, Wang, and me, there was a second Cambodian rifleman. A third, a tall, weather-beaten man, probably a veteran fighter with the Khmer Rouge, stood on the tailgate and held onto one of the bare roof supports. We had a motorcycle escort, a round-faced heavy-set man who carried himself with the easy confidence of a professional soldier. Like many Cambodian nationals, he was clearly of pure Chinese descent. He wore a red-rimmed medal bearing a picture of Mao Tse-tung on his chest. We guessed that he was a defector from the Cambodian army.

There was no longer any need to conceal our faces from the Cambodian villagers. The mass meeting of the day before had made us well-known in the area. As we rattled along the straight dirt road in the mid-afternoon sunshine, we waved to the peasants and got waves of good luck in return. Several times boys on bicycles looked idly at the passing Jeep, did a double-take, and started pedaling furiously after us, trying to catch up.

Now that the departure ceremonies were over, we could concentrate on getting safely to Route 1. The riflemen did not seem particularly alert, so Beth and I divided the horizon between us and watched for planes or helicopters. Mike sometimes would borrow Beth's glasses and help keep watch. We were traveling through flat, open country, with occasional groves of coconut palms and an occasional hamlet or isolated farmhouse.

Ba's eyes were sharper than ours. Before we could make it out, he saw a speck ahead, among the palm trees just above the horizon. "Helicopter!" he said. The driver turned quickly off the road into a farmyard. Peasants ran from the house and, after a few words with the guerrillas, helped guide the Jeep under the elevated house. Ba led us out behind into a grove of banana palms, where we crouched in the cover of the broad leaves and used our sarongs for camouflage. Three helicopters swept in a broad arc that came within a mile or so of us and then headed away. We waited another twenty minutes. Ba warned us once more that our instructions had changed in case of attack: We were to run away from the guerrillas, show ourselves, and wave our white flags. But the danger passed, and we drove on.

Twice we made rest stops at villages, killing time so that we would reach our rendezvous point with a motorbike squad at dusk as planned. At one stop we sat under a thatch-roofed pavilion, with Ba and Wang blocking us from a crowd of curious villagers and explaining over and over that we were friendly news correspondents being taken to safety after living several weeks with the soldiers of the Liberation Front. Despite the explanations, there were some signs of hostility. A dumpy gray-haired farm woman carrying a mattock saw the crowd and lumbered up toward the excitement. "Americans?" she said in amazement when she was told what was going on. She raised the mattock above her head as if to chop us to pieces, and the gesture was only about half joking, until some men grasped her arms and calmed her down. A boy in a clean white shirt with a bandage over one eye made his way through the crowd and stared hard at us for several minutes. Mike took a chance on his understanding Vietnamese and asked. "You've been wounded, haven't you?" "Yes, fighting the American aggression," he said, as if he would like to kill us on the spot.

The second stop was in a farmhouse, where the family was eating dinner. As we sat inside the doorway waiting for darkness, the old grandmother got out her wooden box of the makings for chewing betel nut and had her after-dinner high, while the children took turns outside at the bottom of the ladder scuffing around in my big Western shoes.

A few miles further on, we found the new Japanese motorbikes, one for each of us and each with its Cambodian driver. We all got on behind and took off in the dusk, with the Chinese soldier leading the way along winding paths through forests and over narrow dike roads between the rice paddies. We sometimes traveled as fast as twenty-five miles an hour and then would slow suddenly to take a bump or splash through a flooded section where the warm water, heated by the day's sun, swished over our feet.

For a time, we traveled with headlights on, and I could see the line of lights strung out ahead and behind on the twisted path. Then the Chinese guide stopped briefly to order lights out, and we went on by bright moonlight. After three hours on the motorbikes, we stopped where a row of trees along the roadside gave some cover. Ba and one of the Cambodians drove ahead, their rifles slung on their shoulders. Mike asked Wang where we were. "Two hundred meters from Route 1," he said. "They've gone to see if the way is clear."

The scouts returned with a favorable report, and a few minutes' ride took our line of motorbikes onto a broad curve of the paved highway and across to a row of shops on the other side. We parked under the extended front roof of a restaurant, to get the bikes out of the moonlight. The scouts had awakened the proprietor, and presently he came out with some hot tea and Chinese pastry. As we had our final snack, Mike could overhear Ba and Wang trying to persuade the restaurant owner to let us sleep there until dawn. But life for him was dangerous enough as it was, serving government soldiers in the daytime and guerrillas at night, and he didn't want to risk being known as the man who put up three Americans who had been living with the Liberation forces. Someone settled the matter by finding an empty pavilion down the road and some straw mats to roll out on the floor for a bed.

The parting was emotional. Ba and Wang took turns embracing each of us, and we promised to try to find one another sometime after the war. Our last words were, "What time is it?" "Ten minutes to eleven," Ba said, and the guerrillas rode off into the night.

At dawn, we watched the highway begin its regular changing of owners, now that the guerrillas were gone. First a few men and women came walking along on their way to work in a nearby village. A South Vietnamese military Jeep came racing along for a quick inspection to see that the route was clear for the new day. An hour or so later, normal traffic began, including bicycles, motorbikes, pedicabs and an occasional group taxi racing along from Saigon toward Phnom Penh. Little was moving in the other direction. The heat mounted as we stood waiting in the sun. Another hour passed, and we breathed the dust and fumes of the road traffic. Monks from a nearby pagoda brought us tea, but it helped only momentarily. We couldn't decide whether the white flags were a help or a hindrance. A group of Cambodian students stopped and asked what we were doing there. We told them we were American news correspondents and that our car had broken down and we were trying to get back to Saigon. They stood and talked, saying first that they welcomed American and South Vietnamese help to drive out the Communists, then the bombs had been falling like rain and the South Vietnamese had looted their homes and stolen their money and clothing. We couldn't be sure whose side they were on. When they moved on at last, we rolled up our truce flags and put them away. By now it was mid-morning, and there had been no sign of a ride. After forty days in the quiet and security and relative comfort of rural Cambodia, with the guerrillas making all the decisions, life outside seemed suddenly noisy and dangerous and unpleasant. I asked Mike, "What if we had been held captive for two years instead of a few weeks? Can you understand how a released prisoner blinks his eyes at the light and says, 'I want to go back'?" I felt a sadness and nostalgia for the close community we had enjoyed, much like the choking wave of sadness I had felt as a young man in the merchant marine when the ship sailed off without me after my first short trip.

But the feeling of melancholy passed quickly as soon as we got our first ride, in the back of an open South Vietnamese army truck, and I began to think of returning to my family and writing our story of what the other side was like in this poorly-understood Indochina war. Our next ride was with a twenty-four truck convoy of South Vietnamese army trucks, returning empty after carrying men and supplies to Phnom Penh. We crowded into the cab of one of them and told the driver we were journalists who had gotten caught in a mortar attack and had lost our luggage. We looked straight ahead at every checkpoint and were not challenged once. The convoy took us right into Saigon, where we caught a cab to Mike's house.

After a bite to eat and a quick wash, I went to the USO and placed a call to my home in Washington, where it was 4 A.M. The call went through immediately, and I heard the operator say, "I have a call from Richard Dudman in Saigon." There was a gasp at the other end, and then I could hear Helen's voice saying over and over, "Richard! Richard! Richard!"

epilogue

The story of the forty days must speak for itself. I have tried to set forth what happened, as completely and objectively as possible, and to tell as much as I could about the guerrillas and their movement on the basis of our unusual but admittedly narrow glimpse behind the scenes of the little-known "other side" of the Indochina war.

I have made only two deliberate omissions. Mike, Beth, and I agreed to withhold the exact location of our release. We felt that this would be considered military security information by the guerrillas. We thought it important to avoid giving away their military secrets, both because of the possible effect on other news correspondents who were still missing and might still be held captive, and also because we had meant what we said when we told the guerrillas we were journalists and not spies. The only other omission has been the true names and permanent addresses of our guerrilla escorts. They gave them to us in an unexpected expression of trust and asked us to keep them to ourselves. They asked us to withhold nothing else.

Why were we released? Only after reaching the United States did I learn about the deluge of appeals that flooded the North Vietnamese and the National Liberation Front in Hanoi and Paris and Prince Sihanouk in Peking. Senators, foreign diplomats, scholars, leaders of the peace movement, and fellow newsmen wrote and cabled to their contacts on the other side, assuring them that we were honest reporters and should be released at once. Wilfred Burchett, whom I had come to know at the Paris peace talks, happened to be in Peking for an interview with Prince Sihanouk when we were captured. He had completed his interview but was still in Peking and returned immediately to Sihanouk's headquarters to urge our release. It probably helped that our capture was treated as major front-page news by *The Washington Post*, which Sihanouk reads regularly, and the *International Herald Tribune*, read by the Vietnamese Communists in Paris.

The *St. Louis Post-Dispatch* moved quickly and was willing to do anything to obtain my release. Even the idea of offering a ransom was considered, although this was quickly rejected as unworkable. Joseph Pulitzer, Jr., the editor and publisher, instructed Evarts A. Graham, Jr., the managing editor, to try all possible avenues. Under their direction, Marquis Childs, the columnist, who is contributing editor of the *Post-Dispatch*, flew to Paris and spent a week seeing diplomats and others with connections on the other side. Thomas W. Ottenad, who was acting chief

of the Washington Bureau in my absence, coordinated
many of these efforts. The newspaper prepared copies of
everything I had ever written about the Indochina war and
sent them to our daughters, Janet and Martha, in Paris for
delivery to the North Vietnamese mission.

These appeals must have had their effect, but it should
be noted also that the Vietnamese Communists have usually released prisoners only with a clear political purpose. In
our case, we were freed just two weeks before President
Nixon's self-imposed deadline for the withdrawal of U.S.
forces from Cambodia. Any honest reports of what had
been happening on the other side could not help but offset
the official information out of Phnom Penh, Saigon, and
Washington about the success of the U.S. invasion, the
weakness of the enemy, and the allegedly unified spirit of
the Cambodian people in supporting the Lon Nol regime
and opposing the Communist invaders.

What about the other seventeen news correspondents
still missing in Cambodia? Whenever the Vietnamese Communists had released prisoners it had been on a token
basis, never in wholesale numbers. Only nine U.S. prisoners
of war had been freed, and they had been in three widely-
spaced groups of three each, always with an evident political purpose. Our best reading of the situation was that our
release meant nothing one way or the other about the
status of the other seventeen. We made the most sensible
assumption, that they were still alive, and sent Sihanouk a
joint cablegram the day we arrived in Saigon. He replied
that he would try to learn their whereabouts and arrange
for their release. I have followed this up with correspon-
dence with Sihanouk, with copies to the North Viet-

namese, particularly in behalf of Welles Hangen of the National Broadcasting Company and Robert Anson of *Time* magazine. Anson was freed after being held three weeks, but there has been no word of Hangen at this writing.

Officials of the American Embassy in Saigon asked us for any information that might suggest new efforts to obtain the release of the other missing newsmen. We had been told that our release had come just as plans were being made to send a U.S. military raiding party in after us. We were glad that the rescue attempt never was made in our case, since we probably would have been killed in the process. Our advice was to avoid any military or even diplomatic efforts to free the missing correspondents. Any such moves by the United States government, we said, would do no good and would strengthen the suspicions of the Communists that the newsmen actually were espionage agents. We urged specifically that the CIA and other intelligence agencies avoid asking questions about the missing newsmen. We reminded the officials that our biggest problem had been to convince the guerrillas that we were not CIA spies. All appeals for the release of American news correspondents, we said, should be left to foreign intermediaries, private American citizens and groups, and possibly members of Congress, but certainly the executive branch should keep out of the matter. Some of the American officials in Saigon seemed surprised to hear this advice, but I found in Washington that its good sense was well understood at the Department of State. A further suggestion for any moves in behalf of the missing correspondents was that appeals be addressed to Prince Sihanouk. Although his precise role in the fighting in Cambodia was not clear, he was the nominal head of the Liberation Front and any appeal directed to Hanoi could be considered offensive.

Embassy officials in Saigon also wanted to put us through a "debriefing." We declined, on the ground that our first responsibility was to our newspapers. When pressed, I made the further point that we had spent forty days denying that we were working for the CIA and did not intend to reverse that position now.

Back in Washington, I accepted an invitation from Secretary of State William P. Rogers to discuss the experience after I had finished writing a series of articles for the *Post-Dispatch*. He kept me for two and one-half hours, and I found him an excellent listener. I spent another afternoon with twenty-five senators in a closed-door session arranged by Senator J. William Fulbright, chairman of the Foreign Relations Committee.

One of my first tasks on reaching this country was to arrange for a translation of the safe-conduct pass given us by the guerrillas to use if necessary while making our way back to Saigon. An official at the Cambodian Embassy was good enough to put it into English. Dated June 14 and bearing an illegible signature of the "Commander of Region 203," it said that, "having awakened those prisoners," he had decided to release them and to request the forces of the Cambodian Front to "grant facilities to those people in order to join their own camp." The Cambodian official said he was not familiar with that use of the word "awakened" but supposed that it meant "brainwashed." I knew there would be a certain amount of criticism and skepticism about our findings and recommended to my editors that we publish the translation rather than risk having it come out later as something we had suppressed. The widely syndicated articles were favorably received, however. There were hundreds of commendatory letters and only about ten complaints.

Unexpectedly, I found that I had lost twenty-five pounds in forty days. I felt strong and vigorous, and my belt had been taken up only two holes. But when I got to a scales I realized how much flesh I had lost from my arms and legs and shoulders. The reason, of course, was the rice diet, filling but not very nutritious. We had been eating exactly the same food as the guerrillas, but they had consistently eaten more of it, with smaller bodies to maintain.

In addition to the weight loss, there was a delayed after-effect. I came down with a serious tropical disease just as I finished writing the series of articles on the Cambodian experience. It was caused by a bacterial organism endemic in the soil in parts of Indochina. Two weeks in the hospital, followed by two months' vacation to regain strength and weight, resulted in complete recovery.

I expect to return to Indochina on future assignments to continue reporting the course of the war.

A word about our missing belongings: Some of my credentials had been delivered to the American Embassy in Saigon, but my watch and our cameras and Mike's tape recorder must be in the hands of South Vietnamese troops, who had, indeed, attacked the house where we had stayed the first few nights and where our papers and other belongings had been cached. The borrowed car, when last seen was in the possession of a Cambodian province chief. Our typewriters, which were in the car, probably became his, too.

As a final note, I had hoped that the letter I wrote to my wife would show up eventually. But if it was ever mailed, it has not yet arrived. I should not be surprised at this. I know from personal observation that the guerrillas have other things on their minds than carrying the mail. But even without any word of assurance, Helen stood firm throughout my absence in the conviction that sooner or later I would return safely home.

Washington, D.C.
February, 1971